Also by Paula Deen

Paula Deen: It Ain't All About the Cookin'

Paula Deen Celebrates!

Paula Deen & Friends: Living It Up, Southern Style

The Lady & Sons Just Desserts

*The Lady & Sons, Too!: A Whole New Batch
of Recipes from Savannah*

The Lady & Sons Savannah Country Cookbook

Paula Deen

Christmas
with
Paula Deen

Recipes and Stories
from My Favorite Holiday

Simon & Schuster

NEW YORK LONDON TORONTO SYDNEY

B12640190

SIMON & SCHUSTER
1230 Avenue of the Americas
New York, NY 10020

First Simon & Schuster hardcover edition October 2007

SIMON & SCHUSTER and colophon are registered trademarks
of Simon & Schuster, Inc.

Photographs on pages xii and 136 by Marcy Black for *Cooking with
Paula Deen* magazine. Photographs on pages 8, 112, and 154 by
Mac Jamieson for *Cooking with Paula Deen* magazine. All other
photographs are from the author's personal collection and are used
with her permission.
Much of the material in this book has previously appeared in *The Lady
& Sons Just Desserts, Paula Deen & Friends,* and *Paula Deen Celebrates!*
Owing to limitations of space, acknowledgments of permissions
will be found on page 202.

For information about special discounts for bulk purchases,
please contact Simon & Schuster Special Sales at
1-800-456-6798 or business@simonandschuster.com.

Designed by C. Linda Dingler

Manufactured in the United States of America

10   9   8   7   6   5   4   3   2   1

Library of Congress Cataloging-in-Publication Data
Deen, Paula H.
Christmas with Paula Deen : recipes and stories from my favorite
holiday / Paula Deen.
p.   cm.
1. Christmas cookery.   2. Christmas—United States.   I. Title.
TX739.2.C45D44   2007
641.5'686—dc22   2007035261

ISBN-13: 978-0-7432-9286-3
ISBN-10:   0-7432-9286-3

Acknowledgments

It's so nice that the people in my life don't change too much; if you've read my other books, you'll recognize a lot of these names! So thank you, more than I could ever say:

First, to my husband, Michael Groover, who proposed to me on Christmas Day and gave me the best present I could have ever asked for—himself.

To my boys, Bobby and Jamie; my daughter-in-law, Brooke, and grandbaby, Jack; the Groover kids, Anthony and Michelle, and Michelle's husband, Daniel Reed; my baby brother, Bubba, and his new bride, Dawn; my wonderful niece, Corrie, and nephew, Jay, and Dawn's sons, Iain and Trevor; and my beloved Aunt Peggy Ort. What would Christmas be without y'all?

To my parents, Corrie and Earl Hiers, and my Grandparents Hiers and Grandparents Paul. You taught me the real meaning of Christmas.

To my wonderful staff at The Lady & Sons, especially Dora Charles, who's been with me since the beginning; Rance Jackson, who keeps the kitchen running; my general manager, Dustin Walls; and executive kitchen manager, Scott Hopke. You're my family, too.

To Theresa Luckey and Brandon Branch, my left and right hands.

To Martha Nesbit, my collaborator on *Paula Deen & Friends* and *Paula Deen Celebrates!,* and to Sherry Suib Cohen, who collaborated on my memoir.

To Phyllis Hoffman, who publishes my beautiful magazine, *Cooking with Paula Deen,* and to her wonderful staff.

To my manager, Barry Weiner; my literary agent, Janis Donnaud; Gordon Elliott, executive producer of my television shows; and Nancy Assuncao, my publicist.

To my friends at the Food Network.

To publisher David Rosenthal; associate publishers Deb Darrock and Aileen Boyle; my publicist, Tracey Guest; and everyone at Simon & Schuster, especially my editor, Sydny Miner, and her assistant, Michelle Rorke.

And to all my fans—I love y'all.

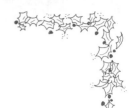

In memory of my two grandmothers,
Grandmomma Hiers and Grandmomma Paul

Because of y'all, my cookbooks were born.

Contents

Christmas with Paula Deen

Paula Deen.

Merry Christmas, Y'all

Hey, y'all!

Christmas is one of my most favorite holidays, and I love the run-up just as much as I do the Big Day itself. Maybe even more; I think the anticipatin' is the best part. How many times have we all been more excited unwrapping a present than about what was in the box, like my grandbaby Jack? His first Christmas, he had way more fun with the boxes and ribbons than he did with what was inside them!

Still, I hope you enjoy what's inside my little Christmas gift to you. I'm big on tradition: My family wouldn't stand for a Christmas dinner without a big piece of beef, or a party without my momma's eggnog. But comes time to make dinner or bake my Christmas cookies, I'm pawing through stacks of torn-out magazine pages and cookbooks to find those recipes I turn to again and again. So I've gone through all my books and put together this collection of my most treasured recipes and memories for the holiday season to share with you, grouping them by occasion. You'll find a few new dishes, a sprinkling of new holiday stories, and some family pictures you might not have seen before.

So Merry Christmas, y'all; and best dishes and best wishes from me and my family to yours.

Paula Deen

Don't Ever Mess
with Christmas

If ever I'm tempted to go to a glamorous, exotic place for Christmas—just my husband, Michael, and me—just in time I'll remember the rule I made when I was very young: Never mess with the holidays. Always be with the people you love, as many of them as you can round up.

No matter what, I always got everyone nuts trying to get us home for the holidays, wherever we were: I can remember when Jimmy Deen (my boys' father) and I had just moved to Savannah. I'll tell you, I missed my hometown of Albany, Georgia, something fierce. By hook or by crook, this Southern gal was going home for Christmas: I would get me and my kids and my husband to Albany. We'd been planning to leave Christmas Eve, but would you believe it started snowing early in the day and Savannah ended up with seven inches of snow! My son Jamie and my niece, Corrie, had gone ahead and were waiting for us in Albany. Now, Southern towns aren't so good about preparing for snowstorms, and that half-foot of white stuff about shut down Savannah. *Nothin'* was moving—not the automobiles, which had turned into bumper cars, not

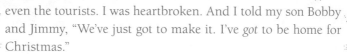

even the tourists. I was heartbroken. And I told my son Bobby and Jimmy, "We've just got to make it. I've *got* to be home for Christmas."

All the kids were jumping for joy. When had they ever seen that much white powder from the sky? But me? I was devastated. Enjoy a Christmas so far away from my Aunt Peggy and people I loved? Impossible. But, next day, that Georgia sun came out shining, that old snow melted, and we did get home to Albany.

One time, when my boys were still very little and we were living in Columbus, Georgia, we had *seventeen* inches of snow. That was really the first time I'd ever seen a snowstorm, and even I had to admit it was so gorgeous. My kids had the best time playing in that snow, and it was then that I was first introduced to snow cream. I am telling y'all the truth, there is nothing better. We were all outside playing, and Ettie May, the housekeeper who lived across the street from us, hollered, "Come on over here, Miss Paula, and eat some snow cream." I scooped up the fresh, cold, white powdery stuff and stuffed it in my mouth, and it was the best treat I'd ever in my whole life tasted. The last time it snowed on the Deen family was in New York around Christmastime a couple of years ago. I was filming my show and it began snowing. I went outside with a big old blue bowl and just filled it up with solid handfuls of snow (being careful to avoid the yellow snow from the passing parade of doggies!). I added a bit of sweetened condensed milk and a couple of spoonfuls of vanilla, mixed it together, and soon the whole crew and I were eating the best homemade snow cream ever invented. It was the sweetest Christmas present on the planet!

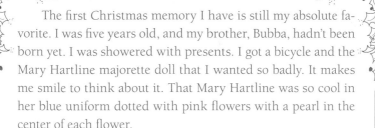

The first Christmas memory I have is still my absolute favorite. I was five years old, and my brother, Bubba, hadn't been born yet. I was showered with presents. I got a bicycle and the Mary Hartline majorette doll that I wanted so badly. It makes me smile to think about it. That Mary Hartline was so cool in her blue uniform dotted with pink flowers with a pearl in the center of each flower.

In our house there were always snow-white lilies, flickering red candles, pomegranate wreaths, and balls of kissing mistletoe. There was gold ribbon everywhere. Aunt Peggy taught me to make our Christmas more fragrant than any other time of the year by preparing a mix of fresh fruit peels (apple, pear, and citrus), apple cores, and bay leaves, plus a few ground-up cinnamon sticks. We'd simmer it all in some water on the stove for hours, bringing fragrance to our holiday home.

Later on I heard about a strange holiday bird called a turducken. A turducken is a turkey, a duck, and a chicken stuffed one inside the other. You have the butcher debone the turkey (except for the legs and the wings), the duck, and the chicken. You cut 'em down their backs, then you lay the turkey breast-side-down, the duck breast-side-down on top of the turkey, and then the chicken breast-side-down on top of the duck. You can choose to stuff the inside bird alone or slather stuffing on top of each bird. Then you take those birds and you pin and tie them back together so that it looks like only one big turkey and roast it for the richest, most impressive main dish ever.

The Christmas stocking was always the best part for me: I loved to dig for all the little gifts in it. Sometimes it meant a ring, a bracelet, or a small doll, but it always meant fruits and nuts. Oranges, apples, Brazil nuts, and walnuts were the stock-

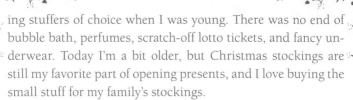

ing stuffers of choice when I was young. There was no end of bubble bath, perfumes, scratch-off lotto tickets, and fancy underwear. Today I'm a bit older, but Christmas stockings are still my favorite part of opening presents, and I love buying the small stuff for my family's stockings.

I so remember the last Christmas before I was married. I was seventeen and it was a bummer.

Momma always put up the tree one week before Christmas, and most of our presents were already wrapped and under the tree by December 23. One day, Momma went to the grocery store and I said to myself, *This is the perfect time for me to go in there and look at all my gifts.*

Very carefully, I snuck into the living room, opened every box with my name on it, pulled out the contents, and then slipped 'em back in their boxes. Carefully, and with a heavy heart, I put the ribbons back on. You would never have guessed that anybody had ever been in those boxes.

Well, when I got through lookin', I was so angry. There was nothing in none of those boxes that I really wanted. But I learned a valuable lesson: Some things are better left wrapped. Some things need to be a surprise.

It was also the same Christmas that Momma went out and bought her own presents. I always knew Daddy would get Momma *something,* but Momma never got what she really wanted. So this one particular Christmas, Momma went out and bought herself everything she wanted, wrapped it, and put it under the tree. Lo and behold, this same Christmas, my daddy did a little bit better with his shopping. He'd bought her a mink stole, and a set of diamond wedding bands was hidden in the folds of that mink stole.

So, we get up Christmas morning, and I know what's waitin' for me, and that ruins everything. Momma, on the other hand, got gifts under the tree that she had bought herself, so she's pretty excited. Well, she opens the first box, and it had a beautiful green negligee set that she'd bought, and she slips it on and she's sittin' there, lookin' like a queen. Then Daddy pulls out this big box from behind the couch and hands it to Momma. She opens it, and it's the mink stole with the diamond-ring bonus. Well, you'd think she'd be happy, but Momma felt so bad because she had bought herself these gifts, and then Daddy had gone out and bought her the world. What's more, her gifts now so outweighed what her children had gotten. Still, I can remember her sittin' there in the living room wearing that negligee with the new fur wrap right on top of it.

For a lot of reasons, none of us was real happy. I had the feeling that if only I hadn't looked at my presents, they would have magically been a lot better. Momma was so embarrassed that she'd one-upped Daddy, but I must admit she still enjoyed every bit of the fur, and the diamond rings, which Jamie's wife, Brooke, now proudly wears.

I personally never again opened a Christmas gift before its time. Some things are worth waitin' on.

The last few Christmases, Michael and I have been either moving into or out of a house, so we especially appreciate Christmas with our family in our own home, just like my daddy always knew was the best kind. I do love this holiday easily as much as I did when I was a little girl, although I've got to say, I haven't gotten a Mary Hartline doll in years. Are you listening, Michael?

New Year's is a special holiday of its own, but I always

Brooke Deen, Jamie Deen, Aunt Peggy (Peggy Ort), Paula Deen, Bubba Hiers, Anthony Groover, and Bobby Deen.

think of it as an extension of the Christmas season. I don't want you to think I'm flaky and woo-woo superstitious, but when that holiday week rolls around, I can't help but be true to the memory of my grandfather Paul, who was a very superstitious man, especially around Christmastime. For instance, I was never allowed to have the goldfish I desperately wanted because he thought they were bad luck. Black cats were no friends to him, and you couldn't get him to walk under a ladder if there was the finest steak and a bottle of Jack Daniel's on the other side of it waitin' for him. And Lord knows, we kids knew better than to open an umbrella in the house.

Today? My whole family usually makes it to my house on Christmas, and also New Year's Day, when I burden them with some superstitions of my own. Even if they hate and despise greens, they've got to have at least one bite of turnip greens, so they'll have financial success all the next year. I always serve the greens along with rice and black-eyed peas with hog jowl because we Southern dames are sure the black-eyed peas bring luck and, believe it or not, those hog jowls promise health.

There is just no way I'm going to mess with Christmas.

Foreground: Paula Deen and Michael Groover.
Background: Bobby Deen, Jamie Deen, and Bubba Hiers.

'Tis Better
to Give . . .
Gifts of Food

There was one Christmas after we left The Lady restaurant at the Best Western and were waiting for The Lady & Sons on West Congress Street to open that found me and the boys unemployed. I was down to about $200 (what I had when I started The Bag Lady!), and I said to the boys, "There's nothin' that I can buy y'all for that kind of money that you don't already have. Why don't we share this with a child?" And the boys, bless them, said, "Momma, that is just perfect. We would love to do that."

So we found a little boy whose mother agreed to let us deliver his presents in person. We went to Wal-Mart and spent every penny of the $200; that child was going to have himself a bunch of stuff! The three of us walked up the steps to the front door of the house with our arms full of boxes; I was wearing a big sweatshirt over black leggings, and a cap. The little boy was waiting at the window, and when he saw me he said to his momma, "Oh, Momma! Look! An elf!"

It was a wonderful Christmas, and if you went back and asked my boys, they'd say it was one of their favorite Christmases, too.

Oven Caramel Corn

This is positively addictive. Put about 2 cups in a clear plastic bag and tie with a beautiful Christmas bow.

> 7 to 8 quarts popped popcorn
> 2 cups unsalted peanuts, shelled pumpkinseeds,
>   and/or sunflower seeds
> 1 cup light brown sugar
> 1 cup (2 sticks) butter or margarine
> 1 teaspoon salt
> ½ cup light corn syrup
> 1 teaspoon maple-flavored pancake syrup
> 1 teaspoon vanilla extract
> 1 teaspoon baking soda

1. Preheat the oven to 250°F. Spray rimmed cookie sheets or jelly roll pans with vegetable oil cooking spray.

2. Place the popcorn and your choice of nuts and/or seeds into a very large bowl. In a medium saucepan, combine the sugar, butter, salt, syrups, and vanilla. Bring to a boil over medium-high heat and continue boiling for 5 minutes, stirring constantly. Remove from the heat and add the baking soda. The mixture will bubble up. Stir vigorously until the mixture is smooth.

3. Pour the hot syrup over the popcorn mix. Stir until

the popcorn is coated. This is messy; take your time and use a long-handled spoon.

4. Spread the coated popcorn in the prepared pans. Bake for 1 hour, stirring several times. The mixture will be very sticky.

5. Remove the popcorn from the oven and allow to cool for 15 minutes. Break big hunks apart while the mixture is cooling. When cooled, the sugars will have candy-coated the popcorn. Store in large, airtight plastic containers.

MAKES 7 TO 8 QUARTS

Icebox Fruitcake

*What are the holidays without fruitcake?
I don't make traditional fruitcake like my grandmother made.
Instead, I make this unbelievably easy stir-together
fruitcake and put it into mini loaf pans for gift giving. This
recipe has appeared before, but I wanted you to have
it again in case you missed it!*

> One 14-ounce can sweetened condensed milk
> One 16-ounce bag miniature marshmallows
> One 16-ounce box graham crackers, crushed
>   to crumbs
> 4 cups chopped pecans
> One 3.5-ounce can flaked coconut (1⅓ cups)
> Two 8-ounce packages chopped dates
> One 16-ounce jar maraschino cherries, well
>   drained, halved
> ½ cup bourbon

1. Spray 10 mini loaf pans with vegetable oil cooking spray.

2. In a 2-quart saucepan, heat the milk and marshmallows together over low heat. Stir constantly (condensed milk scorches easily!) until the marshmallows are melted. Remove the mixture from the heat. Combine the cracker

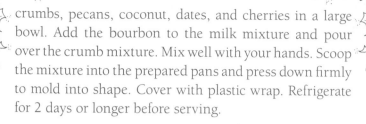

crumbs, pecans, coconut, dates, and cherries in a large bowl. Add the bourbon to the milk mixture and pour over the crumb mixture. Mix well with your hands. Scoop the mixture into the prepared pans and press down firmly to mold into shape. Cover with plastic wrap. Refrigerate for 2 days or longer before serving.

MAKES 10 MINI LOAVES

Mama's Divinity

My momma made these every Christmas, and I do the same. Decorate the just-made candies with red and green sprinkles; they'll stick when the candy hardens.

Remember not to make these candies on a rainy or humid day—they won't harden.

4 cups sugar

1 cup light corn syrup

¾ cup cold water

3 egg whites

1 teaspoon vanilla extract

1 cup chopped pecans

1. In a heavy saucepan over medium heat, stir together the sugar, corn syrup, and water. Stir only until the sugar has dissolved; do not stir after this point. Cook the syrup until it reaches 255°F on a candy thermometer, bringing it to the hard-ball stage.

2. While the syrup is cooking, beat the egg whites until stiff in the large bowl of an electric mixer. When the candy reaches 255°F, carefully wrap the handle of the saucepan with a rag if necessary so you won't burn yourself, and pour a slow, steady stream of syrup into the stiffly beaten egg whites, beating constantly at high speed.

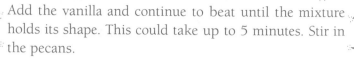

Add the vanilla and continue to beat until the mixture holds its shape. This could take up to 5 minutes. Stir in the pecans.

3. Using 2 spoons, drop the divinity onto waxed paper, using one spoon to push candy off the other. This may take a little practice because the technique is to twirl the pushing spoon, making the candy look like the top of a soft-serve ice cream. If the candy becomes too stiff to twirl, add a few drops of hot water. You will need to work fast when making this type of candy. In fact, when it's time to twirl, it might not hurt to have a friend around.

MAKES 50 TO 60 PIECES

Fruited Rice Curry Mix

This goes well with roast pork or chicken.

1¼ cups raw white rice

2 teaspoons curry powder

2 beef bouillon cubes, crushed, or 2 teaspoons
    granulated bouillon

½ teaspoon salt

¼ cup slivered almonds

2 tablespoons golden raisins

¼ cup chopped dried mixed fruit

Combine all of the ingredients in a small bowl and mix well with your fingers. Place the mixture in a sandwich-size resealable plastic bag and attach this recipe: Combine the contents of this package with 2½ cups water and 2 tablespoons butter in a 2-quart saucepan. Bring to a boil, cover, reduce the heat to low, and simmer for 20 minutes.

MAKES 3 CUPS, ABOUT 6 SERVINGS

Greek Salad Dressing

*By all means include the recipe; your friends
are going to want to keep this on hand at all times in the
fridge. After you shake the dressing, pour it into an attractive
bottle (or bottles) with a stopper.*

> ½ cup olive oil
>
> ¼ cup canola oil
>
> ⅓ cup fresh lemon juice (about 3 lemons)
>
> 1 teaspoon salt
>
> ¼ teaspoon pepper
>
> 1 clove garlic, minced
>
> ¾ teaspoon dried oregano
>
> ¼ teaspoon sugar

Place all of the ingredients in a pint jar with a tight-fitting lid. Shake well. Store in the refrigerator. When ready to use, allow the dressing to come to room temperature and shake well.

MAKES A LITTLE MORE THAN 1 CUP

Chocolate Cheese Fudge

The afternoon I finished testing this recipe, I took a plate of the fudge outside to the park to share with some of my lady friends. As they were oohing and aahing over the fudge, one of them said, "Oh, my goodness, Paula, it's wonderful."

Her mouth dropped open after I told her the fudge was made with Velveeta cheese. "You're sh—ing me!" one of them said, which is not the language these ladies normally use! After all, this is the South.

I hope that when you serve it, you have as much fun as I did. This one is definitely a "Don't Miss!"

> ½ pound Velveeta cheese, sliced
>
> 1 cup (2 sticks) butter
>
> 1 teaspoon vanilla extract
>
> 1 cup chopped nuts
>
> Two 16-ounce packages confectioners' sugar
>
> ½ cup cocoa

1. Spray lightly the bottom of a 9-inch square baking pan with vegetable oil cooking spray.
2. Over medium heat, in a saucepan, melt the cheese and butter together, stirring constantly until smooth. Remove from the heat. Add the vanilla and nuts.

3. In a large bowl, sift together the sugar and cocoa. Pour the cheese mixture into the sugar-cocoa mixture, stirring until completely mixed. The candy will be very stiff. I have found it is easier to do the final mixing with my hands.

4. Using your hands, remove the candy from the bowl and press evenly and firmly into the pan. Because of the amount of butter in this recipe (which you must use), I like to pat the top of the candy with a paper towel to remove excess oil. At this point, you may want to refrigerate it until firm, depending on how quickly you want to serve it. Thirty minutes will usually do the trick. Cut into squares.

MAKES ABOUT 36 SQUARES

For the most wonderful, creamy, melt-in-your-mouth peanut butter fudge you'll ever eat, simply leave out the cocoa and add 1 cup creamy peanut butter. Melt the cheese and butter together, then add the peanut butter and stir until smooth. Proceed as directed in the original directions. I can never seem to make up my mind as to whether I want to add nuts. So, after placing the candy in the pan and patting it out, I will usually sprinkle and press nuts on top of half the pan of candy. That way, I've got the best of both worlds!

Salty Dogs

*O*ne of those fun, messy, no-cooking recipes
that's great for the children.

One 11-ounce package butterscotch chips
1 cup marshmallow crème
½ cup nonfat instant powdered milk
1 teaspoon vanilla extract
½ bag caramel candies (see Note)
2 tablespoons milk
2 cups salted cocktail peanuts, coarsely chopped

1. Melt the butterscotch chips in a glass bowl in a microwave on high (100%) for 2 minutes. Remove and stir in the marshmallow crème and powdered milk. Add the vanilla and stir well. The mixture will be very thick. At this point, I use my hands, kneading the mixture almost like I would bread dough. Roll walnut-sized pieces of the mixture into the shape of your little finger. Place on waxed paper to set.

2. Now, here comes the messy part. Melt the caramels and milk together in a glass dish in a microwave on high for 1½ to 2 minutes. Remove from the microwave and stir well. Roll the fingers in the melted caramel, being careful that it's not so hot *these* fingers will burn *your* fingers. Roll

immediately in chopped nuts, placing the fingers back on waxed paper to harden. If you like, you may dip these in melted chocolate, and you would swear you were eating a Baby Ruth!

NOTE: I use approximately half a bag (22 pieces) of Brach's Milk Maid Rich & Creamy Caramels. You will be melting these caramels, and you will find your melted caramel will thicken as it cools, so you may find it necessary to pop it back in the microwave to loosen it up again. Or you can sit the bowl of melted caramel over hot water to keep it at the right consistency. This would demand extra attention if children are making the candy.

MAKES ABOUT 20 FINGERS

Chocolate Brickle

This quick and delicious candy will definitely satisfy that sweet tooth.

> 1 cup (2 sticks) butter
>
> 1½ cups packed light brown sugar
>
> 1½ cups mixed cocktail nuts (peanuts, almonds, cashews, etc.)
>
> 1 teaspoon vanilla extract
>
> One 12-ounce package semisweet chocolate chips

1. Grease well a 13 by 9 by 2-inch baking pan and set aside.

2. Cook the butter and sugar together in a heavy saucepan over medium heat for 5 minutes, stirring constantly with a wooden spoon. Add the nuts and continue cooking and stirring for an additional 2 to 3 minutes. Remove from the heat, add the vanilla, and pour into the baking pan. Sprinkle the chocolate over the top. As the chocolate begins to melt, gently spread it with a knife.

3. Refrigerate for 20 to 30 minutes, until the chocolate has set and the candy is hard to the touch. You may cut it into squares or invert the pan, tapping on the back with a wooden spoon to release the candy, and break into pieces. Store in an airtight container, unrefrigerated.

MAKES ABOUT 50 PIECES

Vanilla Extract

Homemade vanilla extract is so much better than a store-bought extract and is wonderfully easy to make. I always keep a jar in the cupboard, and give it as gifts to my favorite bakers.

Split 2 vanilla beans lengthwise, then cut them in half crosswise. Put the beans, including any seeds that may fall out, in a clean glass jar. Add ½ cup of bourbon, seal the jar, and give it a vigorous shake. Put in a cool, dark cupboard for 2 weeks and shake it well every day. After 2 weeks, let the extract sit undisturbed for 2 more weeks. It is ready to use after that. If you keep replenishing the extract that you use with an equal amount of bourbon, the beans should last you for at least a year, or longer if you use less extract.

Someone gave me little baby food jars filled with these flavored butters, and I loved the idea so much, I wanted to pass it along to you!

Orange-Ginger Butter

This is terrific with coffee cake or muffins, and is also delicious smeared on broiled fish.

½ cup (1 stick) butter, softened

3 tablespoons orange marmalade

¼ teaspoon grated fresh ginger (the kind in the
    jar is fine)

Combine the ingredients in a small bowl. Pack into a small crock or baby food jar with a decorative lid. Or roll in waxed paper into a log and twist the ends. Chill thoroughly. Wrap in colorful paper.

MAKES ABOUT ¾ CUP

Cinnamon-Honey Butter

*I serve this the morning after Christmas
on homemade waffles.*

½ cup (1 stick) butter, softened
2 tablespoons honey
½ teaspoon ground cinnamon

Combine the ingredients in a small bowl. Pack into a small crock or baby food jar with a decorative lid. Or roll in waxed paper into a log and twist the ends. Chill thoroughly. Wrap in colorful paper.

MAKES ABOUT ½ CUP

Herb Butter

*Delicious on homemade bread. Killer slathered
over grilled steak or chicken.*

> ½ cup (1 stick) butter, softened
> 1 clove garlic, minced
> 1 teaspoon dried parsley flakes
> ½ teaspoon dried basil
> ½ teaspoon dried thyme

Combine the ingredients in a small bowl. Pack into a small crock or baby food jar with a decorative lid. Or roll in waxed paper into a log and twist the ends. Chill thoroughly. Wrap in colorful paper.

MAKES ABOUT ½ CUP

When giving gifts, use everyday objects in unexpected ways. Take some silk fabric and cut it into squares with pinking shears. Place the gift in the middle, then draw up the four corners and tie with a bow. Put cookies or cheese straws on a pretty antique plate and wrap securely with plastic wrap. Tie up the plate with a pretty ribbon and tuck a sprig of greenery—cedar, magnolia, wax myrtle, or boxwood—into the bow.

Lemon-Dill Rice Mix

This is particularly good with seafood, although I also like it with baked chicken.

1½ teaspoons grated lemon zest, dried

½ teaspoon dried minced onion

2 chicken bouillon cubes, crushed, or 2 teaspoons
    granulated bouillon

1 teaspoon dried dill weed

½ teaspoon salt

1¼ cups raw white rice

Combine all of the ingredients in a small bowl and mix well. Place the mixture in a sandwich-size resealable plastic bag and attach this recipe: Bring 2½ cups water and 1 tablespoon butter to a boil in a 2-quart saucepan. Add the contents of this package. Reduce the heat to low, cover, and simmer for 20 minutes.

MAKES 3 CUPS, ABOUT 6 SERVINGS

Russian Spiced Tea Mix

This is fun for really young children. They can measure and mix the ingredients, and could even be invited to "tea" by the recipient!

> One 3-ounce jar Lipton Sweetened Iced Tea Mix
>
> One 21.1-ounce container Tang
>
> 1 tablespoon ground cinnamon
>
> 1 tablespoon freshly grated nutmeg
>
> 1 tablespoon ground allspice

Combine all of the ingredients in a medium bowl and mix well with a metal spoon. Store in small plastic containers or glass jars with tight-fitting lids. Attach this recipe: Use 2 heaping teaspoons in 6 ounces of hot water for hot tea or 2 heaping teaspoons in 6 ounces of cold water for a refreshing summer beverage over ice.

MAKES 5 CUPS, ABOUT 60 SERVINGS

You know, sometimes you really don't realize what an impression a homemade gift makes on somebody. Jamie told me one day, "Momma, do you remember when at Christmastime, you'd go out and buy those little glass jars and you'd fill 'em with all your homemade candy and put a ribbon on 'em and that would be my gift to my teachers? I would be so proud. I remember my chest puffing out when the teacher would say, 'Jamie, thank you so much. That was the most wonderful candy I have ever eaten.' Momma," he said, "you will never, never know how proud those homemade candies made me feel."

When you don't have much money, a simple gift of food delivered in a brown paper bag that you have sponge-painted with a Christmas tree or holly leaf can send such a personal message of sharing and caring.

Peppermint Bark

You can find red and green Chinese food takeout cartons at your local party supply store or online. Line the cartons with gold tissue paper and pack them with this simple but delicious candy to give as gifts.

Peppermint candy canes

18 squares white chocolate (1 ounce each)

Peppermint extract (optional)

1. Line a rimmed cookie sheet with parchment or waxed paper. Place the candy canes in a heavy-duty plastic bag and hammer into ¼-inch chunks or smaller. You should have about 1 cup.

2. Melt the chocolate in a double boiler over simmering water until smooth, or melt in the microwave in a 2-quart glass dish. Microwave on high (100%) for 1 minute, stir, and microwave on high for 10 seconds more. If necessary, microwave on high for an additional 10 seconds, and stir until the chocolate is melted and smooth.

3. Combine the candy cane chunks with the melted chocolate. Add 1 drop of peppermint extract, if desired. Pour the mixture onto the prepared cookie sheet and place in the refrigerator for 45 minutes or until firm. Remove from the cookie sheet and break the bark into irregular pieces, like peanut brittle.

MAKES ABOUT 6 CUPS

Just as April showers bring May flowers, the Christmas season brought homemade goodies from the Deen boys. Only the look my teachers got when I managed to sit still for ten minutes rivaled the excitement in their eyes when I walked in bearing the fruits of Mom's labors.

JAMIE DEEN

Christmas Cookies

Brooke Deen, Jamie Deen, Paula Deen, Jack Deen, Jay Hiers, Michelle Groover, Michael Groover, Corrie Hiers, Bubba Hiers, and Bobby Deen.

It's just not Christmas without Christmas cookies, and as far as I'm concerned, you can never have enough recipes. Here are some of my favorites, old and new. There are super-easy cookies like my Willie Wonder Wafers, classics like Ginger Cookies and Sand Tarts, and elegant goodies like my Savannah Bow Ties.

Now's the time to get your kids into the kitchen with you. If they're too young to help you bake, let them decorate rolled and cut-out Cream Cheese Cookies, or Gingerbread Boys and Girls. There's no better way to make sweet memories.

Cookie Hints

1. Begin with a good, heavy cookie sheet. Dark cookie sheets can produce a dark, almost burned bottom. Always keep two good baking sheets in your kitchen inventory. You will be able to keep a constant flow of cookies going into the oven. This will also allow the pans to cool in between batches of cookies. Never put cookie dough on a really hot pan.

2. Be consistent in the size you make your cookies.

3. Place the cookie sheet on the center rack of the oven.

4. Because most ovens have "hot spots," you may find that one side is browning faster than the other. Simply give the pan a 180-degree turn halfway into the cooking time, placing what was the front of the pan in the rear.

5. If your cookies are coming out too flat, you might try adding a little more flour. If that doesn't work, try chilling the dough in the refrigerator.

6. If you don't have a cooling rack, transfer cookies to a waxed paper–lined surface to cool.

7. I find that a thin metal spatula works better

than a thick plastic spatula for removing cookies from the pan.

8. Store cookies in an airtight container instead of a cookie jar for a longer shelf life. If it's a sticky cookie, place a sheet of waxed paper between the layers of cookies. I don't like to use a cookie tin except to transfer from one location to another for a short period of time.

9. For crisp cookies that have gone soft, place on a cookie sheet in a low oven (225° to 250°F) for a few minutes.

10. To keep a soft cookie from staling, throw a piece of bread in the container along with the cookie. A slice of apple works great also.

11. If you like a dense cookie, mix by hand. If you prefer a lighter, crisper cookie, beat with an electric mixer. This will put more air into the dough.

12. Parchment paper is a great pan saver. If cut to fit the baking sheet, it eliminates greasing the pan and cleanup.

13. Adjust your baking time on cookies to suit your taste. If you like a softer, chewy cookie, cut back on baking time. If you like a crisper cookie, increase baking time.

Paula's Ultimate Oatmeal Cookies

I created this recipe on my television show. I could have eaten the whole plateful myself—and I just about did!

½ cup (1 stick) butter, softened

½ cup vegetable shortening

1½ cups packed light brown sugar

2 eggs

½ cup buttermilk

1¾ cups all-purpose flour

1 teaspoon baking soda

½ teaspoon salt

1 teaspoon baking powder

1 teaspoon ground ginger

1 teaspoon freshly grated nutmeg

1 teaspoon ground cinnamon

¼ teaspoon ground cloves

½ teaspoon ground allspice

2½ cups quick-cooking oatmeal (not instant!)

1 cup raisins

1½ cups chopped walnuts

1 teaspoon vanilla extract

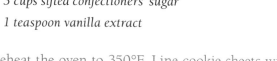

BROWN BUTTER ICING:

½ cup (1 stick) butter
3 cups sifted confectioners' sugar
1 teaspoon vanilla extract

1. Preheat the oven to 350°F. Line cookie sheets with parchment paper or nonstick baking mats.

2. Using an electric mixer, cream together the butter, shortening, and sugar at low speed until fluffy. Add the eggs and beat until the mixture is light in color. Add the buttermilk and mix to combine.

3. Sift together the flour, baking soda, salt, baking powder, ginger, nutmeg, cinnamon, cloves, and allspice. At low speed, gradually add the dry ingredients. Using a spatula, fold in the oatmeal, raisins, walnuts, and vanilla, blending well. Drop by rounded teaspoonfuls 1½ inches apart onto the prepared cookie sheets. Bake for 12 to 15 minutes.

4. While the cookies are baking, make the icing: In a small saucepan, heat the butter over medium heat until golden brown, stirring occasionally. Remove the saucepan from the heat; stir in the sugar and vanilla. Stir in enough water (3 to 4 tablespoons) to make an icing of drizzling consistency.

5. Remove the cookies to wire racks to cool. Drizzle with Brown Butter Icing while the cookies are still warm.

MAKES ABOUT 5 DOZEN

Chocolate Sandwich Cookies

*This makes a lot of cookies, but these never seem
to last long. They're a big favorite with kids of all ages,
and I'd leave some out for Santa to enjoy with a glass of milk.*

Two 18.5-ounce packages devil's food cake mix

4 eggs, lightly beaten

⅔ cup vegetable oil

One 8-ounce package cream cheese, softened

½ cup (1 stick) butter, softened

3 cups sifted confectioners' sugar

½ teaspoon vanilla extract

1. Preheat the oven to 350°F. Line cookie sheets with parchment paper.

2. In a large mixing bowl, combine the cake mix, eggs, and oil. Beat with an electric mixer at low speed until completely combined. The batter will be very stiff. Pinch off pieces of batter and roll into 1-inch balls. Place 1 inch apart on the prepared cookie sheets and flatten slightly with fingertips. Bake for 8 to 10 minutes, until a slight indentation remains when lightly touched. Remove immediately from the cookie sheets with a spatula and cool on wire racks.

3. In a small glass mixing bowl, combine the cream

cheese and butter until completely blended. Gradually add the sugar and vanilla and mix at low speed until the icing is smooth. Spread icing on half the cookies and top with the remaining cookies. Store in the refrigerator in large resealable plastic bags.

MAKES ABOUT 4 DOZEN SANDWICHES

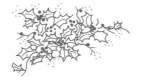

Ginger Cookies

The smell of these spicy cookies baking says "Christmas" to me. Even the littlest kitchen elves can help you shape the cookies and roll them in sugar.

¾ cup vegetable shortening

1 cup sugar

1 egg

¼ cup molasses

2 cups sifted all-purpose flour

2 teaspoons baking soda

1 teaspoon ground cinnamon

1 teaspoon ground ginger

½ teaspoon ground cloves

½ teaspoon salt

Additional sugar, for rolling cookies

1. Preheat the oven to 350°F. Line cookie sheets with parchment paper or nonstick baking mats.

2. Using an electric mixer at low speed, cream the shortening and sugar until thoroughly combined. Add the egg and molasses and beat until completely incorporated.

3. Sift together the flour, baking soda, cinnamon, ginger, cloves, and salt and add to the mixture. Stir until combined.

4. Roll the dough into balls about 1 inch in diameter. Roll the balls in sugar. Place 1½ inches apart on the prepared cookie sheets. Flatten the balls slightly with fingertips. Bake for 12 minutes. Cool on wire racks. Store in resealable plastic bags.

MAKES ABOUT 3 DOZEN

Benne Seed Cookies

*Benne seed is another name for sesame seed.
This is an old favorite low-country recipe given to my friend
Martha Nesbit by a Savannah caterer, the late Sally Sullivan.
It makes dozens of tiny, crisp brown-sugar cookies
about the size of a quarter. For a sweet gift, fill an oversize
teacup or mug with cookies, wrap in cellophane, and tie it
with a beautiful ribbon. Present it with a special tea
(there are wonderful specialty Christmas teas available
at this time of year).*

> 1½ cups sesame seeds
> One 1-pound package light brown sugar
>   (2½ cups, packed)
> 1½ cups (3 sticks) butter, softened
> 2 large eggs
> 2 cups all-purpose flour
> 1 teaspoon baking powder
> ¼ teaspoon salt
> 2 teaspoons vanilla extract

1. Preheat the oven to 350°F.

2. If you're using raw sesame seeds, place the seeds in a single layer on a baking sheet. Place in the oven for

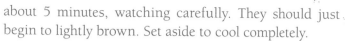

about 5 minutes, watching carefully. They should just begin to lightly brown. Set aside to cool completely.

3. Lower the oven temperature to 300°F. Line cookie sheets with parchment paper.

4. Using an electric mixer, cream the sugar, butter, and eggs until very light, about 5 minutes. Sift the flour, baking powder, and salt. Add to the butter mixture and stir with a spatula until combined. Add the vanilla. Stir in the cooled sesame seeds. Drop the batter by ½ teaspoonfuls onto the prepared cookie sheets, 1 inch apart. It takes just a dab of batter to produce quarter-size cookies. They will spread into perfect circles during baking.

4. Bake until very brown but not burned at the edges, 14 to 15 minutes. *Important:* Let the cookies cool *completely* on the parchment paper, then peel them away from the paper. Store between layers of waxed paper in an airtight container. These cookies freeze well in tins. They will crumble in a plastic freezer bag.

MAKES ABOUT 12 DOZEN

Sand Tarts

*My Grandmomma Paul used to make these all the time.
My baby brother, Bubba, and I used to beg my momma
to make them, and she would promise to get the recipe
but never did. Finally, when Bubba was ten he called
Grandmomma himself and got the recipe!*

> 1 cup (2 sticks) butter, softened
> ½ cup confectioners' sugar, plus more for coating
>   baked cookies
> 1 teaspoon vanilla extract
> 1¾ cups all-purpose flour, plus more for
>   dusting hands
> 1 cup pecans, chopped into very small pieces

1. Preheat the oven to 275°F. Line cookie sheets with parchment paper.

2. Using an electric mixer at low speed, cream the butter and sugar until smooth. Beat in the vanilla. At low speed, gradually add the flour. Mix in the pecans with a spatula.

3. With floured hands, take out about 1 tablespoon of dough and shape it into a crescent. (Continue to dust your hands with flour as you make more cookies.) Place the cookies 1 inch apart on the prepared cookie sheets.

Bake for 45 minutes. Dust with additional confectioners' sugar while still warm. Cool completely on wire racks and store in airtight containers.

MAKES 2½ DOZEN

Raisin Puffs

*These are Martha Nesbit's son Zack's favorite cookies.
They've been sent along on many a church choir tour.
Aunt Mary Lou Haney, of Reynoldsville, Pennsylvania,
provided the recipe.*

> 2 cups raisins
>
> 1½ cups sugar
>
> 1 cup (2 sticks) butter, softened
>
> 1 teaspoon vanilla extract
>
> 3 cups all-purpose flour
>
> 1 teaspoon baking soda
>
> ½ teaspoon salt
>
> Additional sugar for rolling cookies

1. Preheat the oven to 350°F. Line cookie sheets with parchment paper or nonstick baking mats.

2. Place the raisins and ¾ cup water in a small saucepan, and simmer gently until the raisins have absorbed most of the water and are soft, about 5 minutes. Drain.

3. Using an electric mixer at low speed, cream the sugar, butter, and vanilla until thoroughly combined. Sift together the flour, baking soda, and salt. Stir the dry ingredients and raisins into the butter mixture with a spoon. The batter will be crumbly.

4. Gather about a tablespoon of dough in your fingers and squeeze so dough holds together. Roll into walnut-sized balls. Roll in sugar and place 1½ inches apart on the prepared cookie sheets. Bake for 12 to 15 minutes, until lightly browned and puffed. Transfer to wire racks to cool. Store in airtight containers, as these are quite fragile and have a tendency to fall apart if jostled.

MAKES ABOUT 4 DOZEN

Lace Cookies

This is a lacy, crisp, buttery cookie. The batter spreads considerably due to the high butter content and the small amount of flour in the recipe. These are so good that one of our young friends, Cameron Curlee, has requested them in her Christmas stocking instead of candy! Now, that's a good cookie!

½ cup (1 stick) butter or margarine

1 cup sugar

1 egg

1 teaspoon vanilla extract

3 tablespoons all-purpose flour

½ teaspoon salt

1 cup quick-cooking oatmeal
  (not instant!)

1. Preheat the oven to 350°F. Line cookie sheets with aluminum foil, parchment paper, or nonstick baking mats.

2. Using an electric mixer at low speed, cream the butter and sugar until thoroughly combined. Add the egg and vanilla and mix well. Stir in the flour, salt, and oatmeal, mixing well with a spoon. Drop by teaspoonfuls

2 inches apart onto the prepared cookie sheets. Bake for 5 to 8 minutes, until lightly browned. Let cool completely before removing from the sheets; peel cookies away from the lining.

MAKES 2½ DOZEN

Magnolia Lace Trumpets

*To make these cookies into a very special gift, I tie thin
satin ribbons in different colors into a bow around
each cookie, then nestle the cookies in tissue paper
in a box tied with matching ribbons.*

½ cup sugar

½ cup (1 stick) butter

⅓ cup dark corn syrup

¾ cup all-purpose flour

½ teaspoon ground ginger

1 tablespoon Irish cream liqueur (optional)

FILLING:

1½ cups vegetable shortening

½ cup (1 stick) butter

1½ cups sugar

1 egg white

2 teaspoons vanilla extract

½ cup hot milk

1. Preheat the oven to 350°F. Line a cookie sheet with
aluminum foil or a nonstick baking mat. Lightly grease
the foil. (If you don't grease the foil, the cookies will stick
and be ruined.)

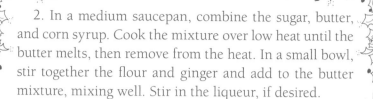

2. In a medium saucepan, combine the sugar, butter, and corn syrup. Cook the mixture over low heat until the butter melts, then remove from the heat. In a small bowl, stir together the flour and ginger and add to the butter mixture, mixing well. Stir in the liqueur, if desired.

3. Drop the batter by rounded teaspoonfuls 3 to 4 inches apart onto the prepared cookie sheet. Bake only 2 or 3 cookies at a time because they will spread, and you must work quickly to form the cones before they cool and become brittle. (If the cookies do become too brittle to roll, put them back in the oven for a minute to soften.)

4. Bake for 9 to 10 minutes, until bubbly and golden brown. Quickly invert the cookies onto another cookie sheet and wrap each cookie around the greased handle of a wooden spoon or a metal cone, available from specialty cookware stores. When the cookie is set, slide it off the spoon or cone; let cool on a wire rack.

5. While the cookies are cooling, make the filling: Using an electric mixer, cream together the shortening and butter. Add the sugar and beat well. Add the egg white and vanilla; beat thoroughly. Add the hot milk, 1 tablespoon at a time, and beat until creamy. Put the filling into a pastry tube fitted with the star tip and fill the cookies.

6. To store: Place unfilled cookies in a single layer in an airtight container. Store at room temperature in a cool, dry place for up to 3 days, or freeze unfilled cookies for up to 3 months. Thaw the cookies and fill.

MAKES 2½ DOZEN

Monster Cookies

*Christmas didn't roll around at our house that we didn't
have M&M cookies; this is a variation of that recipe.
You're reading the ingredients list right:
There is no flour in the recipe.*

6 eggs

One 1-pound package light brown sugar
   (2½ cups, packed)

2 cups granulated sugar

½ teaspoon salt

½ teaspoon vanilla extract

One 24-ounce jar creamy peanut butter

1 cup (2 sticks) butter, softened

8 ounces M&M's

8 ounces chocolate chips (two thirds of
   a 12-ounce bag)

½ cup raisins (optional)

4 teaspoons baking soda

9 cups quick-cooking oatmeal (not instant!)

1. Preheat the oven to 350°F. Line cookie sheets with
parchment paper or nonstick baking mats.

2. In a very large mixing bowl, combine the eggs and sugars. Mix well. Add the salt, vanilla, peanut butter, and butter. Mix well. Stir in the M&M's, chocolate chips, raisins (if using), baking soda, and oatmeal.

3. Drop by tablespoonfuls, 2 inches apart, onto the prepared cookie sheets. Bake for 8 to 10 minutes. Do not overbake. Let stand for about 3 minutes before transferring to wire racks to cool. When cool, store in large resealable plastic bags.

MAKES ABOUT 6 DOZEN

Savannah Bow Ties

I call this "my ultimate cookie recipe."
I just think it's the best.

1 sheet frozen puff pastry from a 17.25-ounce
   package (I like Pepperidge Farm.)
½ cup almond paste
1 egg, separated
¼ cup packed light brown sugar
2 teaspoons milk
Flour for dusting the work surface
Granulated or coarse sugar, for sprinkling

CHOCOLATE DIPPING SAUCE:

¾ cup granulated sugar
2 tablespoons cornstarch
¼ teaspoon salt
Six 1.5-ounce milk chocolate bars
2 cups whipping cream
1 egg yolk, beaten
½ teaspoon vanilla extract

1. Let the puff pastry stand at room temperature for 20
minutes, or until easy to roll. Preheat the oven to 400°F.

Line cookie sheets with aluminum foil, parchment paper, or nonstick baking mats.

2. Crumble the almond paste in a small mixing bowl. Add the egg yolk, brown sugar, and milk. Beat with an electric mixer at medium speed until well combined. The filling will be very stiff.

3. Unfold the pastry on a lightly floured surface. Roll out into a 14-inch square. Cut the square in half with a fluted pastry wheel.

4. Drop dollops of filling uniformly over one of the rectangles of dough. Spray a piece of waxed paper with vegetable oil cooking spray and use it to press the filling evenly over the dough. Spray the waxed paper as often as necessary to prevent the filling from sticking.

5. Place the remaining rectangle on top of the filling. Using a fluted pastry wheel, cut the dough crosswise into fourteen 1-inch-wide strips, then cut each strip in half crosswise to make 28 pieces. Twist each piece twice. Place the twists about 2 inches apart on the prepared cookie sheets. Brush the twists with lightly beaten egg white. Sprinkle with granulated sugar.

6. Bake for 12 to 15 minutes, until golden. Transfer to wire racks to cool.

7. While the cookies are cooling, make the Chocolate Dipping Sauce: In a saucepan, stir together the sugar, cornstarch, and salt. Crumble the chocolate bars in one at a time. Gradually stir in the cream. Cook, stirring, over low heat, until the chocolate is melted. In a small bowl, combine ½ cup of the hot chocolate sauce with the egg

yolk. Add the yolk mixture to the pot and cook, stirring, until the sauce comes to a boil. Remove from the heat. Stir in the vanilla and pour into a serving bowl. Any remaining sauce can be poured into custard cups, refrigerated, and served as pudding.

8. Serve the cookies with Chocolate Dipping Sauce.

MAKES **28** COOKIES

Date-Nut Sticks

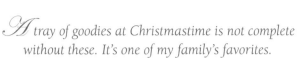

A tray of goodies at Christmastime is not complete without these. It's one of my family's favorites.

¾ cup (1½ sticks) butter

2 eggs, beaten

2 cups sugar

One 8-ounce package chopped dates

2 teaspoons vanilla extract

1 cup chopped nuts

1½ cups Rice Krispies

3 cups finely grated coconut

In a saucepan over medium heat, melt the butter. Add the eggs, sugar, and dates. Bring to a boil, reduce the heat to low, and cook 10 minutes, stirring constantly. Remove from the heat. Stir in the vanilla, nuts, and Rice Krispies. Let cool and shape into finger-sized sticks. Roll in the coconut.

MAKES 45 STICKS

The Cookie Swap

People may claim to be counting calories and carbs, but few people in their right mind will turn down a homemade cookie, and you can always find people willing to chuck their diets to attend a Cookie Swap!

A Cookie Swap is held early enough in the season so that cooks still have time to use their new recipes for their friends and family.

Guests bring a plate of their best cookies, along with copies of the recipe. Guests sample the cookies and take home the recipes they like the most. Of course, polite guests take home one of *every* recipe so as not to hurt anybody's feelings.

All the hostess has to do is provide a lovely tablecloth and a big centerpiece—showy flowers (hydrangeas, tulips, roses, or sunflowers), perhaps with recipes stuck among the flowers on metal holders. Guests bring their cookies artfully arranged on pretty plates, and the plates are placed on the table. For serving, you can provide small glass or china plates (best) or pretty paper plates (acceptable). Serve lemonade, iced or hot tea, and coffee, although ice-cold milk would certainly be appreciated! The best part of this party (aside from eating cookies!) is that guests are encouraged to take home the leftovers, so there is really no cleanup involved.

Willie Wonder Wafers

I always made these with the boys when they were young because they're soooo easy to make. Just make sure your little ones wash their hands before they start kneading the dough! Sprinkle the cookies with red or green decorating sugar or edible glitter before baking.

> ½ cup (1 stick) butter
> 1 cup packed light brown sugar
> ⅛ teaspoon salt
> 1 egg
> 1 teaspoon vanilla extract
> 3 cups all-purpose flour
> 1 teaspoon baking powder

1. Using an electric mixer, cream together the butter, sugar, salt, egg, and vanilla in a bowl until fluffy. Sift together the flour and baking powder; gradually add to the creamed mixture (the dough will be very dry). Turn out onto a floured board and knead thoroughly until the dough is well mixed and handles easily. Refrigerate overnight.

2. Preheat the oven to 350°F and lightly grease one or more cookie sheets.

3. Roll the dough into logs, slice thin, and place on a cookie sheet. Bake for 8 to 10 minutes, watching very carefully that they don't burn. Cool on wire racks and store in airtight containers.

MAKES ABOUT 6 DOZEN

Cream Cheese Cookies

Get out those cookie cutters, y'all! It's not Christmas without some decorated cut-out cookies on the cookie tray.

> 1 cup (2 sticks) butter, softened
> One 3-ounce package cream cheese, softened
> 1 cup sugar
> 2 egg yolks
> ½ teaspoon vanilla extract
> 2½ cups all-purpose flour

1. Using an electric mixer, cream together the butter and cream cheese. Add the sugar and beat until fluffy. Add the egg yolks and vanilla. Add the flour, stirring, ½ cup at a time. Chill the dough for 30 minutes.

2. Preheat the oven to 350°F and grease one or more cookie sheets. Roll the dough out to ¼-inch thick; cut with cookie cutters. Place the cookies on a cookie sheet and bake for 10 to 12 minutes. Let cool on a wire rack and serve.

MAKES ABOUT 4 DOZEN

Christmas was a happy time at our house when I was a kid, even though we didn't have a whole lot. On a typical Christmas Eve I remember goin' over to Grandaddy Deen and Mama Wray's house for dinner. All of my daddy's side of the family would be there, and we'd exchange small gifts. It's funny, but I don't remember much that was special about the food, except for the snack tray filled with celery and carrot sticks, and olives. Christmas Eve dinner was only Christmassy because we were all together.

The radio station in Albany, Georgia, would always do a "Santa watch," so all the kids would be on a lookout for the sleigh when it flew over. When the DJ announced that Santa had been sighted over Albany, Jamie and I would strain to look out the window to see if we could see Santa and his reindeer.

I totally believed in Santa. My brother and I would leave a plate of cookies and a glass of milk, and wake up to find the cookies had been nibbled on and some of the milk had been drunk. I guess Santa didn't want to fill up at one house, no matter how good Mama's cookies were! And I can remember lying in bed and hearing footsteps on the roof and telling my brother I knew it was Santa—of course, now I know that it was my daddy up there. Didn't everyone's parents do that?

Then there was the year that all the needles fell off the Christmas tree. I guess we all forgot to water the darn thing, and woke up to find we had a big stick with decorated branches!

BOBBY DEEN

Chocolate Meringue Kisses

If you're looking for a lighter option for your Christmas cookie platter, this is a perfect recipe to choose.

>   1 cup confectioners' sugar
>   3 egg whites, stiffly beaten (please use an electric mixer)
>   ½ cup crushed saltine crackers
>   ½ cup chopped walnuts or pecans
>   1 teaspoon vanilla extract
>   One 6-ounce package semisweet chocolate chips (about 1 cup)

1. Preheat the oven to 325°F. Grease cookie sheets.

2. Fold the confectioners' sugar into the stiffly beaten egg whites a little at a time. Fold in the crackers, nuts, and vanilla.

3. Melt the chocolate in a double boiler over hot water and allow to cool slightly. Fold into the egg-white mixture.

4. Drop by rounded half-teaspoonfuls onto the cookie sheet. Bake for 12 minutes. Remove the cookies from the oven and transfer to a wire rack to cool. Store in an airtight container.

MAKES 4 DOZEN

Gingerbread Boys and Girls

*K*ids especially love these. Serve them plain and allow the kids to decorate them with icing piped from a plastic bag with a hole in one corner made with a toothpick. Red, green, and white icing usually suffices for the holidays. Add miniature chocolate chips, jelly beans, sprinkles, and red hots if you like.

¾ cup packed dark brown sugar

½ cup (1 stick) butter or margarine, softened

2 large eggs

¼ cup molasses

3¾ cups all-purpose flour, plus more for dusting
    work surface

2 teaspoons ground ginger

1½ teaspoons baking soda

½ teaspoon ground cinnamon

½ teaspoon freshly grated nutmeg

½ teaspoon salt

Icing:

1 cup confectioners' sugar, sifted

1 tablespoon milk

Food coloring as desired

1. Using an electric mixer at low speed, cream the sugar and butter until thoroughly combined. Add the eggs and molasses and mix until combined. Sift together the flour, ginger, baking soda, cinnamon, nutmeg, and salt. Add the dry ingredients to the butter mixture and combine with a spoon or spatula. Remove the dough from the bowl and wrap in plastic wrap; place in the refrigerator until firm, about 1 hour.

2. Preheat the oven to 350°F. Line cookie sheets with parchment paper. Allow the dough to sit at room temperature for about 15 minutes, until pliable. Take about ½ cup of dough at a time and roll onto a floured work surface until about ⅛-inch thick. Cut out with gingerbread boy and girl cookie cutters. You can reroll the scraps.

3. Using a spatula, transfer the cookies from the work surface to the prepared cookie sheets. Bake for 10 minutes, until just beginning to brown at the edges. Transfer to wire racks to cool.

4. To make the icing: Combine the confectioners' sugar and milk. Divide the mixture into thirds; leave one third white, color one third green, and color the final third red. Decorate by piping eyes, mouths, buttons, and bow ties.

MAKES 18 TO 24 COOKIES, DEPENDING ON THE SIZE
OF YOUR COOKIE CUTTERS

Pecan Dreams

*Taste one of these and you'll see why
we call them dreams!*

1½ cups confectioners' sugar
1 cup all-purpose flour
One 8-ounce package cream cheese
½ cup (1 stick) butter, softened
1 cup chopped pecans

TOPPING:

1 cup whipping cream
2 tablespoons granulated sugar
1 cup Heath Bits o' Brickle Toffee Bits

1. Preheat the oven to 350°F. Lightly grease a 9-inch square baking pan.

2. Stir together the confectioners' sugar and flour in a bowl. Using a pastry cutter or fork, cut the cream cheese and butter into the flour mixture until crumbly. Press the dough into the prepared pan, distributing evenly. Pour the nuts over and press into the dough. Bake for 30 minutes. Remove from the oven and let cool completely.

3. While the base is cooling, make the topping: Whip the cream and granulated sugar together with a handheld electric mixer until stiff; fold in the toffee bits. Spread over the base. Cut into squares. Store in the refrigerator.

MAKES 25 SQUARES

Frosted Pumpkin Bars

These are so moist and delicious!

BARS:

4 large eggs

1⅔ cups granulated sugar

1 cup vegetable oil

One 15-ounce can pumpkin

2 cups all-purpose flour

2 teaspoons baking powder

1 teaspoon cinnamon

1 teaspoon salt

1 teaspoon baking soda

FROSTING:

One 3-ounce package cream cheese, softened

½ cup (1 stick) butter, softened

1 teaspoon vanilla extract

2 cups sifted confectioners' sugar

1. Preheat the oven to 350°F.

2. Using an electric mixer at medium speed, beat the eggs, granulated sugar, oil, and pumpkin until light and fluffy. Sift together the flour, baking powder, cinnamon,

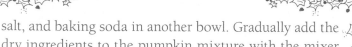

salt, and baking soda in another bowl. Gradually add the dry ingredients to the pumpkin mixture with the mixer at low speed. Mix until thoroughly combined and the batter is smooth.

3. Spread the batter in an ungreased nonstick 13 by 9-inch baking pan. Bake for 30 minutes. Remove from the oven and let cool completely before frosting.

4. To make the frosting: Combine the cream cheese and butter in a medium bowl with an electric mixer until smooth. Add the vanilla. Slowly beat in the confectioners' sugar until smooth. Spread on the cooled pumpkin base and cut into bars. These freeze well.

MAKES 24 LARGE BARS OR 48 SMALLER ONES

*Christmas
Morning*

Opening presents takes a lot of energy, so I sure don't want to fuss in the kitchen on Christmas morning. Try some of the make-ahead recipes here, like the Sausage Swirls or the Praline French Toast Casserole, for a delicious start to the day. And for all of you who were up late putting together toys, make sure there's plenty of hot coffee!

A late breakfast or brunch is also a relaxed way to welcome friends and family during the holidays. I love to show off our beautifully decorated home and our Christmas trees. We've got four: our family tree; one in the living room, with decorations that match our décor; one in the morning room off our kitchen; and one in Michael's and my bedroom. I love lying in bed with the lights from the tree the only light in the room (it's very romantical!). But my favorite tree is the family tree. When the boys were little, I would buy each of them an ornament every year, and put a little piece of tape with the date on the bottom; all those go on that tree, as well as ornaments the boys made for me when they were in school (including a cookie that Bobby made for me in playschool when he was four).

All our trees go up exactly one week before Christmas, and come down one week after. That's the way my momma did it, and her father, Granddaddy Paul, did it, and I'm carrying on the family tradition.

Breakfast Casserole

You surely don't want to be up cooking bacon and eggs on Christmas morning. Preheat the oven, pop this in, and the whole house will wake up to the smell of something yummy. As a matter of fact, you have to make this savory bread pudding the night before so the bread soaks up all the seasoned egg mixture.

5 slices thick-sliced white bread, crust and all,
    buttered and cubed
1 pound mild sausage, cooked, crumbled, and drained
3 cups grated extra-sharp Cheddar cheese
4 eggs
2 cups milk
1 teaspoon dry mustard
1 teaspoon salt
1 teaspoon hot sauce

1. Spray a 1½-quart casserole dish with vegetable oil cooking spray. Place the bread cubes in the casserole. Evenly distribute the sausage over the bread cubes. Sprinkle evenly with the cheese. Combine the eggs, milk, mustard, salt, and hot sauce and mix well. Pour the egg mixture over the bread. Cover with plastic wrap and refrigerate overnight.

2. The next morning, remove the casserole from the refrigerator and allow it to sit on the counter for 15 minutes while you preheat the oven to 350°F. Remove the plastic wrap, place the casserole in the oven, and bake for 1 hour.

SERVES 6 TO 8

Sour Cream~ Butter Biscuits

These biscuits take me back to my days at The Bag Lady. I would put a couple of these in each lunch container for an extra treat! They are wonderful, and so rich you don't need butter, just some honey or jam.

> 2 cups self-rising flour
> 1 cup (2 sticks) butter, softened
> 1 cup sour cream

1. Preheat the oven to 400°F. Grease mini muffin pans.

2. In a bowl, use 2 knives to cut the butter into the flour until they are thoroughly combined. Add the sour cream and stir with a fork until completely mixed.

3. Place spoonfuls of the batter in the prepared muffin pans. Bake for 8 to 10 minutes or until golden. Serve hot.

MAKES ABOUT 3 DOZEN MINIATURE BISCUITS

Sausage Swirls

Two ingredients? We're not kidding! You can't believe how easy and delicious these little numbers are. You can also bake them in advance. Reheat them in a warm oven and they'll taste like you just made them.

Two 8-ounce cans refrigerated crescent dinner rolls
1 pound ground sausage, mild for kids, hot for adults, or sage if you prefer

1. Separate 1 can of dough into 4 rectangles. Firmly press the perforations to seal. Take the uncooked sausage and cut it into 8 chunks. Using 4 chunks of the sausage, spread each of the rectangles with a thin layer (about ⅛ inch thick). Starting at the short end, roll each rectangle tightly into a cylinder. Repeat with the other can of dough and remaining sausage. Place on a plate, cover with plastic wrap, and chill until firm, about 30 minutes, then cut each roll into 4 slices.

2. When ready to bake, preheat the oven to 375°F. Place the sausage swirls ½ inch apart on ungreased baking sheets. Bake for 18 to 20 minutes, until golden brown and the sausage is thoroughly cooked.

MAKES 32 SWIRLS

Mushroom and Sausage Quiche

This makes a huge, rich quiche.

One 9-inch refrigerated piecrust, fitted into a
    9-inch glass pie plate
One 1-pound package ground sausage, crumbled
1 tablespoon butter
½ pound fresh mushrooms, sliced
½ large Vidalia onion, chopped
4 eggs
1 cup sour cream
1 cup cottage cheese, 2% or 4% milkfat
3 tablespoons all-purpose flour
3 tablespoons freshly grated Parmesan cheese
1 teaspoon hot sauce
One 8-ounce package shredded sharp
    Cheddar cheese

1. Preheat the oven to 350°F. Crimp the edges of the crust.

2. In a large skillet, cook the sausage. Drain and set aside. Wipe out the pan and, in the same pan, melt the

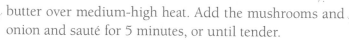

butter over medium-high heat. Add the mushrooms and onion and sauté for 5 minutes, or until tender.

3. Place the eggs, sour cream, cottage cheese, flour, Parmesan cheese, and hot sauce in a food processor and process until smooth, stopping to scrape down the sides of the bowl.

4. In a large bowl, stir together the sausage, mushroom mixture, egg mixture, and Cheddar cheese, and spoon into the piecrust. Cover the edges of the piecrust with aluminum foil to prevent the crust from burning.

5. Bake for 50 to 60 minutes, until golden brown and the center is set. Let cool for 10 minutes and cut into 8 wedges.

SERVES 8

Baked Garlic-Cheese Grits

A Southern favorite. This goes well with seafood, too.

6 cups chicken broth (canned is fine)

1 teaspoon salt

¼ teaspoon pepper

2 cups regular grits

Three 6-ounce rolls Kraft cheese food with garlic, or
   any garlic-Cheddar spread, cut up

½ cup milk

4 eggs, beaten

½ cup (1 stick) butter

1 cup grated sharp Cheddar cheese

1. Preheat the oven to 350°F. Grease a 4-quart casserole dish.

2. Bring the broth, salt, and pepper to a boil in a 2-quart saucepan. Stir in the grits and whisk until completely combined. Reduce the heat to low and simmer until the grits are thick, about 8 minutes.

3. Add the garlic cheese and milk and stir. Gradually stir in the eggs and butter, stirring until all are combined.

4. Pour the mixture into the prepared casserole dish. Sprinkle with the Cheddar cheese and bake for 45 minutes, or until set.

SERVES 12

Spinach and Bacon Quiche

6 eggs, beaten
1½ cups milk
Salt and pepper
2 cups chopped fresh baby spinach, packed
1 pound bacon, cooked and crumbled
1½ cups shredded Swiss cheese
One 9-inch refrigerated piecrust, fitted into a
*   9-inch glass pie plate*

1. Preheat the oven to 375°F.

2. Combine the eggs, milk, and salt and pepper to taste in a food processor or blender. Layer the spinach, bacon, and cheese in the bottom of the piecrust, then pour the egg mixture on top.

3. Bake for 35 to 45 minutes, until the egg mixture is set. Cut into 8 wedges.

SERVES 8

Broiled Parmesan Tomatoes

*A recipe like this, which is quick and easy and delicious,
makes it easy on the hostess. Tomatoes always taste so good
with brunch food, and this recipe takes advantage of the
wonderful canned tomatoes that are always available.
Tomatoes are canned by weight, which means that one
14.5-ounce can might have eight small tomatoes in it,
and the next one might have six. Count on each can
having six tomatoes; better to have leftovers!
Each guest would have one tomato.*

> Three 14.5-ounce cans whole tomatoes, drained
>   (any variety, including Italian plum)
> Salt and pepper
> ½ cup (1 stick) butter
> 1½ cups freshly grated Parmesan cheese

Preheat the broiler. Place the tomatoes in a 13 by 9-inch
flameproof baking dish. Sprinkle with salt and pepper to
taste and top each with a pat of butter. Generously sprinkle the cheese over the tomatoes. Broil for 10 to 15 minutes, until the tomatoes are heated through and the cheese
is bubbly.

SERVES 16

It was coming up on our second Christmas together, and I was dying for a ring, but I thought, *This shaggy river man don't know nothin' about no diamond rings.* I confided in my niece, Corrie, "You know, I'm almost hoping for an engagement ring. I'd so wish I'd get that for Christmas, but I know he would never do that."

And Corrie said, "Well, you *don't* know that."

And then I said, "Well, don't tell anybody that I've said that wish because I don't want people to even dream that I am thinkin' that way."

But I was. This is the way it was with me. Although we were so happy living together, I seem to have just needed Michael to propose and let me know that his intentions were honorable. It almost didn't matter if we got married. I deeply wanted him just to ask, so that I knew he was in there for the long haul, so that I knew he was committed. I needed that like I needed to breathe.

So, on Christmas Eve I noticed at the back of that overflowing tree of gifts that there was a new gift, a big box shaped like a house with a white tag on it. The tag said "Paula" in real big letters.

That gift has just come into this house, but I'm going to pretend like I don't see it, I thought.

The next morning, all the family shows up. Michael and his children have spent the night there with me, so we're already there. Then my children come piling in, as well as Bubba and Corrie. Nick, Michael's brother, and *his* children come in. I was talking and laughing and seeing if anybody wanted something to eat, and finally Michelle, Michael's daughter, came over and said, "Listen, you've got to start opening your gifts. I've got to get to Momma's."

I said, "Me open my gifts? *You* start opening *your* gifts. I'm not worried about my gifts." But I thought, *Well, that was real strange.*

Before I knew it, they'd sat me down in

a chair; they knew I'd be the last one to open gifts because I'm always seeing to everybody else. The room got quiet. I thought, *Why is everybody looking at me? Christmas is for children.*

Well, I wanted everyone else to open their gifts first, as was the custom in my family, especially because I'd bought Michael a magnificent Rolex watch and I couldn't wait to see his face when he unwrapped it. "No one has ever given me a thing in my life," he'd once told me, "maybe not even bought me a meal." So, I was focusing on him and his present and I could barely contain myself.

But Michelle would have none of that. Although each person had a few gifts waiting, she ignored the others with my name on them, went to get the intriguing house-shaped box, and set it down before me.

"*There,*" she said. "We're waiting for you, Paula."

I looked over to where Michael was

propped on the frame of the wet bar. Ernest Hemingway was just standing there grinning.

Well, I opened this box that said "Paula," and in it was another box surrounded by all my favorite candy that I could just eat by the pound: Hershey's Kisses, Snickers—stuff like that. And in a third box, it was the same thing.

Corrie said, "Paula, there's a message in each box. Read it."

So, I went back to the first box, and it said "Paula." The next box had a message that said "I." The next box said "love." The next box said "you." I opened the next box, and it said "Will."

When that durned box said "Will," I said, "No! I mean yes!" I knew what was coming, and so the entire message—it took nine boxes—said, "Paula, I love you. Will you be my wife?"

That last, ninth box held a diamond ring. I'd found a man who gave diamonds? I couldn't believe the ring . . . it was simply

*I finally realized that Michael
was proposing to me!*

magnificent. How could this rugged river
man have such an eye for jewelry? Oh, that
ring. I haven't taken it off since.

It was the most wonderful proposal, so
romantic and so like Michael. He devised
this extraordinary way to do this thing

For once, I'm speechless!

in front of all the people we love, and he never had to open his mouth. *He never had to open his mouth.* They were all in on it, by the way. Corrie had even seen the ring.

It was a blessed Christmas.

Praline French Toast Casserole

*Everyone will love this! It's very rich,
so it goes a long way.*

8 eggs
1½ cups half-and-half
⅓ cup maple syrup
⅓ cup packed light brown sugar
10 to 12 slices soft bread, 1 inch thick

TOPPING:

½ cup (1 stick) butter
½ cup packed light brown sugar
⅔ cup maple syrup
2 cups chopped pecans

1. Generously butter a 13 by 9-inch baking dish.

2. Mix the eggs, half-and-half, maple syrup, and sugar in a large bowl. Place the bread slices in the prepared baking dish and cover with the egg mixture. Cover with plastic wrap and let soak overnight in the refrigerator.

3. Preheat the oven to 350°F. Remove the baking dish from the refrigerator.

4. Make the topping: Melt the butter in a saucepan. Add the sugar and maple syrup and cook for 1 to 2 minutes. Stir in the pecans. Pour the mixture over the bread and bake for 45 to 55 minutes. Allow to sit for 10 minutes before serving.

SERVES 8

The Best
Damn Blueberry Muffin
You'll Ever Eat

Here in Savannah, we love our muffins, and I especially
love these delicately blended, delicious blueberry babies.
Fresh blueberries may be expensive around Christmas,
but they are surely worth it. This is my favorite
blueberry muffin recipe.

> 2 cups all-purpose flour
> 2 tablespoons baking powder
> ½ cup sugar
> ½ cup (1 stick) unsalted butter, melted
> 1 egg, slightly beaten
> ¾ cup whole milk
> 1½ cups fresh blueberries
> ½ cup granulated brown sugar or white sugar

1. Preheat the oven to 350°F. Grease and flour 12 muffin cups.

2. In a bowl, combine the flour, baking powder, and the ½ cup sugar. In another bowl, combine the butter, egg, and milk, and blend well. Pour the wet ingredients

into the flour mixture and, with a spatula, stir until just combined. Do not beat or overmix; it's okay if there are lumps in the batter. Gently fold the blueberries into the batter.

3. Spoon the batter into the muffin cups, filling each cup about two-thirds full. Bake for 10 minutes and remove from the oven.

4. Sprinkle the tops of the muffins with the granulated brown sugar and return the muffins to the oven to bake for an additional 10 to 20 minutes, until the tops are golden brown and a toothpick inserted into the center of a muffin comes out clean. Let cool for about 10 minutes in the pan before turning the muffins out.

MAKES 12 MUFFINS

Orange-Walnut Sunrise Coffee Cake

Perfectly wonderful and perfectly easy.

*One 16.3-ounce can Pillsbury Grands! Flaky Layers
    refrigerated biscuits*

¼ cup finely chopped walnuts

⅓ cup granulated sugar

2 teaspoons grated orange peel

2 tablespoons butter, melted

½ cup confectioners' sugar

*1½ ounces (half a 3-ounce bar) cream cheese,
    softened*

1 tablespoon orange juice, or more as necessary

1. Preheat the oven to 375°F. Grease a 9-inch round cake pan.

2. Separate the biscuit dough into 8 biscuits. Place 1 biscuit in the center of the pan. Cut the remaining biscuits in half, forming 14 half circles. Arrange the pieces around the center biscuit with cut sides facing in the same direction.

3. In a small bowl, combine the walnuts, granulated sugar, and orange peel, and mix well. Brush the butter

over the tops of the biscuits and sprinkle with the walnut mixture. Bake for 20 minutes or until golden brown.

3. Meanwhile, in a small bowl, combine the confectioners' sugar, cream cheese, and enough orange juice for desired drizzling consistency. Blend until smooth, then drizzle over the warm coffee cake. Let cool 10 minutes. Serve warm.

SERVES 8

Gorilla Bread

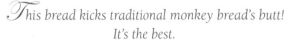

*This bread kicks traditional monkey bread's butt!
It's the best.*

> 1 cup granulated sugar
>
> 1 tablespoon ground cinnamon
>
> ½ cup (1 stick) butter
>
> 1 cup packed brown sugar
>
> One 8-ounce package cream cheese
>
> Two 7.5-ounce cans refrigerated biscuits (10 count)
>
> 1½ cups coarsely chopped walnuts

1. Preheat the oven to 350°F. Spray a Bundt pan with vegetable oil cooking spray.

2. Mix the granulated sugar and cinnamon. In a saucepan, melt the butter and brown sugar over low heat, stirring well; set aside.

3. Cut the cream cheese into 20 equal cubes. Press the biscuits out with your fingers and sprinkle each with ½ teaspoon of cinnamon sugar. Place a cube of cream cheese in the center of each biscuit, wrapping and sealing the dough around the cream cheese.

4. Sprinkle ½ cup of the nuts into the bottom of the Bundt pan. Place half of the prepared biscuits in the pan. Sprinkle with cinnamon sugar, pour half of the melted

butter mixture over the biscuits, and sprinkle on ½ cup of nuts. Layer the remaining biscuits on top, sprinkle with the remaining cinnamon sugar, pour the remaining butter mixture over the biscuits, and sprinkle with the remaining ½ cup of nuts. Bake for 30 minutes. Remove from the oven and let cool for 5 minutes. Place a plate on top and invert. Serve warm.

SERVES 12 TO 15

Almond Danish Swirls

*Crescent rolls? Yes! In this recipe they're rich
and sweet with cream cheese, almonds, and almond glaze.
We modified a recipe from the thirty-fifth Pillsbury Bake-Off
contest cookbook to make individual Danish swirls.
The original recipe was one large Danish. These can be made
the day before and stored in a plastic bag in the refrigerator.
Bring to room temperature before serving.*

> Two 3-ounce packages cream cheese, softened
> 1 teaspoon almond extract
> ½ cup confectioners' sugar
> 1 cup slivered almonds, chopped fine
> Two 8-ounce cans refrigerated crescent dinner rolls
> 1 egg white
>
> GLAZE:
>
> ⅔ cup confectioners' sugar
> ½ teaspoon almond extract
> 4 teaspoons milk

1. In a small bowl, beat the cream cheese, almond extract, and sugar until fluffy. Fold half of the almonds into the mixture.

2. Separate 1 can of dough into 4 rectangles. Firmly

press the perforations to seal. Press or roll each piece of dough to form a 7 by 4-inch rectangle, and spread each with about 2 tablespoons of the cream cheese filling to within ¼ inch of the edges. Starting at the short end, roll each rectangle tightly into a cylinder. Repeat with the other can of dough and remaining filling. Place on a plate, cover with plastic wrap, and chill until firm, about 30 minutes.

3. Preheat the oven to 350°F while the rolls are chilling. Remove from the refrigerator and cut each roll into 4 slices. Place ½ inch apart on ungreased baking sheets.

4. In a small bowl, combine the egg white with 1 teaspoon water. Brush over the swirls. Sprinkle with the remaining almonds.

5. Bake for 18 to 20 minutes, until light brown.

6. While the swirls are baking, combine the glaze ingredients in a small bowl. Cool the swirls for 3 minutes on wire racks placed over a sheet of waxed paper. Drizzle the icing over the warm swirls.

MAKES 32 SWIRLS

Fruit Kebabs

*You can set out the wooden skewers
and fruit and let your guests put these together
themselves, or you can make them yourself.
You can buy wooden skewers at the supermarket
or housewares store.*

> *1 pint ripe strawberries, hulled*
> *1 pineapple, peeled, cored, and cut into chunks*
> *Green and red grapes*

Alternate pieces of fruit on skewers.

MAKES 6 TO 8 SKEWERS

Christmas has always been my favorite time of year. When Bobby and I were younger, we had a special calendar for December, and every day we took down a candy cane and split it, taking us one day closer to Christmas. The excitement was so high by the 24th, we barely slept. Mom and Dad had a rule that we couldn't go to the Christmas tree until they were up; we did that as a family. My mom always loved to share our thrill as we explored what Santa had left behind. Well, I bet for ten or twelve years our folks didn't log five hours' sleep on any Christmas Eve!

Mom always had a special breakfast made the night before; the mornings we spent together with wrapping paper scattered to kingdom come and a belly full of breakfast were just the best.

And then we got older. Dammit.

We started The Bag Lady, a lunch delivery business, in 1989, and for a long time Christmas meant a break from our endless schedule. We were so busy, one year Mom said we couldn't afford and had no time to get a Christmas tree. I could not face the holidays without that simplest of pleasures. The smell of a fresh-cut tree is one of my favorite things, and while I didn't have the money either, we did have a coat rack. So that was it. I strung that rack with a strand of lights and hung a few glass balls from it. One of the most depressing images

*Brooke and Jamie Deen on the deck at
Uncle Bubba's Oyster House.*

from my past has grown to be one of my fondest memories.

Now I am married, and Brooke and I have started our own Christmas traditions. The first Christmas her family came to visit, we spent Christmas morning surrounded by endless mounds of crumpled wrapping paper . . . and I did the cooking. We so look forward to future Christmases when we will hang a special calendar for our children. And to losing sleep on Christmas Eve.

JAMIE DEEN

Christmas
Dinner

My family and I just love Christmas. It's all about family, food, and fun to us.

My daddy would not allow us to be away from the house at Christmas; he always said that children belong at home on Christmas Eve. We never went to our friends or even our grandparents; everybody came to us. Momma would make her wonderful eggnog, and I can hear Momma and Daddy and our friends and family standing around in the kitchen, just laughing and talking.

I keep that tradition, and to make sure it happens, I open our house to everyone in my blended and extended family so we can all have the opportunity to be with our children.

I don't do a lot of variations on my Christmas Day meal. At my house, we are full up with turkey and ham from Thanksgiving, and at the restaurant, we have to cook so many turkeys and hams for Thanksgiving, and throw so many parties with turkey and dressing, that I am just sick to death of turkey by the time Christmas rolls around. All I want is beef. My favorite is the standing rib roast, but let me tell you something: I won't throw away a beef tenderloin, either. And naturally, you have to have a tater—a tater's got to be invited to the table in some shape, form, or fashion.

Christmas Lime Salad with Aunt Peggy's Cranberry Sauce

This is one of those dishes that is just beautiful to see.

> 1 package lemon Jell-O
> 1 package lime Jell-O
> One 20-ounce can crushed pineapple
> One 16-ounce container cottage cheese
> 1 cup mayonnaise
> ½ cup orange juice
> ½ cup pecan pieces
> 1 teaspoon prepared horseradish

Dissolve the Jell-O in 2 cups hot water, then pour into a 13 by 9-inch casserole. Refrigerate until slightly jelled. Add the remaining ingredients and stir gently. Return to the refrigerator until completely set.

SERVES 10 TO 12

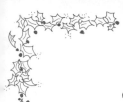

Aunt Peggy's Cranberry Sauce

*O*ur holiday table isn't complete without my Aunt
Peggy Ort's cranberry sauce. This is so easy, y'all,
and a hundred times better than canned.
*If you're using frozen cranberries, you don't have
to thaw them; just throw 'em in the pot straight
from the freezer.*

1 cup water

1 cup sugar

One 12-ounce package cranberries, fresh or frozen

Combine the water and sugar in a medium saucepan and
bring to a boil over medium-high heat. Add the cranberries and return to a boil. Lower the heat to medium and
boil gently for about 10 minutes, stirring occasionally.
Cover, and cool completely at room temperature. Refrigerate until serving time.

MAKES ABOUT 2¼ CUPS

Crab Mousse

One 10.75-ounce can condensed cream of
   mushroom soup
One 8-ounce package cream cheese
1 envelope unflavored gelatin, softened in ¼ cup
   cold water
½ pound lump crabmeat, picked through for shell
   and cartilage
1 cup finely chopped celery
¼ cup chopped green onions, white and
   green parts
1 tablespoon fresh lemon juice
1 teaspoon Worcestershire sauce
¼ teaspoon seasoned salt

1. Grease a 3-cup seafood mold.

2. Combine the soup, cream cheese, and softened gelatin in a glass bowl. Heat for 2 minutes in the microwave, until very hot. Stir well to make sure that the gelatin is completely dissolved and there are no lumps. Add the crabmeat, celery, green onions, lemon juice, Worcestershire sauce, and seasoned salt. Stir gently but thoroughly.

3. Spoon the mixture into the mold and smooth the top. Cover with plastic wrap and chill until firm. When

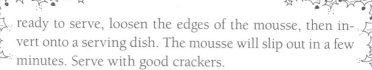

ready to serve, loosen the edges of the mousse, then invert onto a serving dish. The mousse will slip out in a few minutes. Serve with good crackers.

SERVES 8 TO 10

Standing Rib Roast

*This recipe is one of my family's favorites. You can start it
early in the day and finish it when it's time for dinner.
Do not remove the roast or open the oven door from the time
the roast is put in until the final roasting.*

One 5-pound standing rib roast, bone in

1 tablespoon Paula's House Seasoning

1. Allow the roast to stand at room temperature for at least 1 hour. Preheat the oven to 375°F.

2. Rub the roast with House Seasoning. Place the roast on a rack in a roasting pan with the rib side down and the fatty side up. Roast for 1 hour. Turn off the oven and leave the roast in the oven; do not open the door.

3. About 1 hour and 10 minutes before serving time, turn the oven on to 375°F and reheat the roast for 30 to 40 minutes. Remove the roast from the oven and tent with foil. Allow the meat to rest for 25 to 30 minutes before carving.

SERVES 8 TO 10

Soy-Rubbed Tenderloin

This is really so simple. I buy a whole tenderloin when it goes on sale and have it cut in two. I fix one that night and freeze the other for a special occasion.

One 4- to 5-pound beef tenderloin
½ cup soy sauce
Freshly ground black pepper

1. Allow the beef to stand at room temperature for 1 hour. Preheat the oven to 425°F.

2. Place the tenderloin in a 13 by 9-inch glass baking dish and rub all over with the soy sauce. Rub the meat all over with a generous amount of black pepper.

3. Roast the tenderloin for 45 to 50 minutes, depending on the degree of doneness you prefer. (Using a meat thermometer, 125°F is rare; 135°F is medium rare; and 140°F is medium.) Remove from the oven and allow the meat to rest for 15 minutes before you slice it.

SERVES 10 TO 12

Twice-Baked
Potato Casserole

This is such a great dish because you can make it the day ahead. I love to spiff it up at Christmas by adding shrimp (see Variation).

> 8 medium baking potatoes, about 4 pounds
> One 8-ounce package cream cheese, softened
> ½ cup (1 stick) butter, softened
> 2 cups shredded sharp Cheddar cheese
>   (½ pound)
> 1 pint sour cream
> 2 cloves garlic, minced
> 1½ teaspoons salt
> ½ teaspoon pepper
> ¼ cup chopped fresh chives, for garnish
> 6 slices bacon, cooked crisp, drained, and
>   crumbled, for garnish

1. Preheat the oven to 350°F. Pierce the potatoes and place on a baking pan. Bake the potatoes for 1 hour and 15 minutes, until very soft.

2. Peel and mash the potatoes in a large bowl with a potato masher or the back of a fork. Add the cream cheese,

butter, 1 cup of the Cheddar cheese, and the sour cream. Stir well. Add the garlic, salt, and pepper and stir again.

3. Spray a 13 by 9-inch baking dish with vegetable oil cooking spray. Place the potatoes into the dish. The casserole may now be covered with plastic wrap and refrigerated until ready to bake.

4. When ready to bake, preheat the oven to 350°F. Remove the plastic wrap and bake the potatoes for 30 to 35 minutes, until hot. Sprinkle the remaining 1 cup Cheddar cheese over the top of the casserole and return to the oven for about 5 minutes, until the cheese melts. Garnish with the chopped chives and crumbled bacon before serving.

SERVES 10 TO 12

VARIATION:

Twice-Baked Potato Casserole with Shrimp

Prepare the Twice-Baked Potato Casserole through step 2. Melt a tablespoon of butter in a large skillet. Take 1 pound of small peeled, deveined shrimp and sauté them for 30 seconds on each side. Spray a 13 by 9-inch baking dish with vegetable oil cooking spray. Spread half of the potato mixture evenly over the bottom of the dish. Distribute the shrimp evenly over the potatoes and top with the remaining potatoes. Continue with step 4 of the recipe as above.

Crème Fraîche Mashed Potatoes

1 cup plus 2 tablespoons whipping cream

¾ cup sour cream

2 pounds small red potatoes

1 teaspoon salt

One 8-ounce package cream cheese, softened

2 tablespoons roasted garlic (from a jar or homemade)

1 teaspoon Paula's House Seasoning

1 teaspoon Paula's Seasoned Salt

4 tablespoons (½ stick) butter, slivered

¼ cup sliced green onions, green and white parts

1 tablespoon chopped fresh chives

1. Prepare the crème fraîche ahead of time by combining 1 cup of the whipping cream with ½ cup of the sour cream. Cover with plastic wrap and let stand at room temperature for 12 to 24 hours or until thick. Stir well and refrigerate for at least 4 hours. Crème fraîche will keep for up to 2 weeks.

2. Put the potatoes in a saucepan and cover with cold water. Add the salt and bring to a boil. Cook until the

potatoes are tender, 20 to 25 minutes. Drain and peel as soon as they are cool enough to handle.

3. While the potatoes are cooking, preheat the oven to 350°F. Lightly grease a 2-quart round casserole.

4. With an electric mixer, beat the potatoes with the cream cheese, the remaining ¼ cup sour cream, 2 tablespoons whipping cream, the garlic, House Seasoning, and Seasoned Salt. Stir in the butter and green onions. Spread the potatoes in the casserole. Spoon the crème fraîche on top and sprinkle with the chives. Bake until the potatoes are hot, 20 to 30 minutes.

SERVES 8

Sweet Potato Bake

3 cups peeled, cooked, and mashed sweet potatoes
    or yams (about 1½ pounds raw)

1 cup granulated sugar

½ cup (1 stick) butter, melted

2 eggs

1 teaspoon vanilla extract

1 teaspoon ground cinnamon

¼ teaspoon freshly grated nutmeg

¼ cup whipping cream, half-and-half, or
    whole milk

TOPPING:

1 cup light or dark brown sugar

1 cup walnuts, chopped

⅓ cup all-purpose flour

3 tablespoons butter, melted

1. Preheat the oven to 325°F. Grease a 2-quart casserole dish.

2. Combine the sweet potatoes, granulated sugar, butter, eggs, vanilla, cinnamon, and nutmeg. Beat with an electric mixer until smooth. Add the cream and mix well. Pour into the casserole dish.

3. Mix the topping ingredients together in a small bowl with a fork. Sprinkle evenly over the top of the casserole.

4. Bake for 25 to 30 minutes, until the potatoes are hot and the topping is golden.

SERVES 8

Brussels Sprouts
with Onion and Bacon

Not everybody loves Brussels sprouts, which taste and look like sweet little cabbages, but I bet this recipe would change their mind.

½ pound lean bacon, finely diced

1 cup diced yellow onion

2 cloves garlic, minced

2 pounds Brussels sprouts, trimmed

2 cups chicken broth

4 tablespoons (½ stick) butter

1. In a heavy-bottomed pot over medium heat, fry the bacon until crisp. Remove the bacon and drain on paper towels.

2. Sauté the onion and garlic in the bacon grease over low heat until soft, about 3 minutes. Add the Brussels sprouts and stir them around so that they are coated with the bacon grease.

3. Add the broth and cook, covered, over low heat until the sprouts are easily pierced with a fork, about 12 to 15 minutes. Stir in the butter just before serving. Garnish each serving with bacon bits.

SERVES 8

When Whipping Cream:

1. One cup heavy or whipping cream yields 2 cups whipped. Whipping cream and heavy cream are the same. Do not confuse with half-and-half, which cannot be whipped.

2. Avoid overbeating, because you will turn the cream into butter. You can achieve a stiff peak, but don't take it past that point.

3. I use ¼ cup of sugar to 1 cup whipping cream in most all of my recipes. If this is too sweet for you, simply reduce the amount of sugar to suit your taste.

4. Try adding cocoa to whipping cream, with a little extra sugar because chocolate is bitter. Simply add cocoa to the cream and beat as usual.

5. Be sure your bowl and beaters are well chilled and your cream is very cold.

Waterford Chocolate Mousse

*This mousse is rich and delicious.
Serve in a beautiful crystal dish—Waterford recommended.
Okay, maybe you don't have a piece of Waterford crystal.
So how about that beautiful glass dish that we all have that
we purchased from the dime store? You can also pour
the mousse into individual compote dishes,
and top with dollops of fresh whipped cream
and strawberries.*

Six 4-ounce bars Ghirardelli bittersweet chocolate

⅔ cup extra-strong brewed coffee

4 large eggs, at room temperature, separated

1½ cups sugar

2 cups whipping cream

1. Break the chocolate into small pieces; melt the chocolate with the coffee in the top of a double boiler. Using a fork, beat the egg yolks slightly; stir in 1 cup of the sugar and mix well. Add this mixture to the melted chocolate and leave over the heat, stirring until well blended and the sugar is dissolved. Remove from the heat and allow the mixture to cool to the touch.

2. Using a handheld electric mixer, beat the egg whites until stiff but not dry. Fold into the chocolate mixture. Beat the cream with the remaining ½ cup sugar until soft peaks begin to form. Fold into the chocolate mixture. Gently spoon the mousse into your prettiest glass bowl(s) and chill thoroughly.

SERVES 12 TO 15

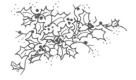

Mama's Eggnog

6 eggs, separated (see Note)

¼ cup sugar

2 cups whipping cream

2 quarts milk

1 cup bourbon

1 tablespoon vanilla extract

Freshly grated nutmeg (optional)

1. In a large bowl, using an electric mixer, beat the egg yolks with ½ cup of the sugar until thick. In another bowl, beat the egg whites with the remaining ¼ cup sugar until thick but not dry. In a third bowl, beat the cream until thick but still soft.

2. Fold the cream into the yolks, then fold in the egg whites. Gently stir in the milk, bourbon, vanilla, and a pinch of nutmeg, if desired. Chill thoroughly before serving.

3. Serve the eggnog in a large punch bowl.

SERVES 8 TO 10

NOTE: Eating raw or lightly cooked eggs carries the risk of contracting a type of food-borne illness caused by salmonella bacteria. Raw eggs should not be eaten by the very young, the very old, pregnant women, or anyone with a compromised

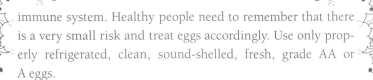

immune system. Healthy people need to remember that there is a very small risk and treat eggs accordingly. Use only properly refrigerated, clean, sound-shelled, fresh, grade AA or A eggs.

*Holiday
Open House*

$\mathcal{W}e$ travel so much these days that Michael and I don't always have time to spend with our friends. A holiday open house is a perfect way to reconnect and bring people together. I serve a mix of savory and sweet nibbles; a house cocktail instead of an open bar makes the hostess's life a little easier. I always offer a nonalcoholic drink, too.

I love antique Christmas ornaments, and I can't pass up an opportunity to add to my collection. One of my best finds was at a yard sale; the people giving the sale had owned an old variety store. In a beat-up old paper box I found a tangle of glass beads. When I was a girl we'd go to the county fair, and I always played the duck game. There was a kiddie pool filled with plastic ducks; you picked one, and the number on the bottom matched the number of the prize. My favorite prizes were the glass bead necklaces, just like the ones in the paper box. Oh, they were beautiful—pink and green and silver. There must have been 150 of them at that yard sale, and I bought every single one. I've hung them on my Christmas trees for years; now they hang from our special family tree.

Tomato Tarts

These tarts smell so delicious when they are cooking, your guests will want to pluck them straight from the pan, but you need to let them cool or you'll burn your tongue! The recipe originally came from Savannah caterer Trish McLeod, but it's been slightly altered. You'll need a biscuit cutter for this recipe; take it with you when you shop for the tomatoes, so your tomatoes and pastry rounds are the same size.

> 1 sheet frozen puff pastry from a 17.25-ounce package
>   (I like Pepperidge Farm.)
> Olive oil
> ½ cup grated white Cheddar cheese
> 4 or 5 Italian plum tomatoes, cut into ¼-inch slices
> Salt and pepper
> 2 tablespoons fresh thyme leaves, chopped fine
> Approximately ½ cup freshly grated Parmesan cheese

1. Preheat the oven to 375°F. Spray a baking sheet with vegetable oil cooking spray. Meanwhile, remove the puff pastry from the freezer and allow to thaw for 20 minutes.

2. Unfold the pastry on the counter and, using a 1½- or 2-inch biscuit cutter, cut out rounds of dough. Place the

puff pastry rounds on the prepared baking sheet. Prick the surface of the pastry with a fork. Brush each round lightly with olive oil and top with a small amount of the Cheddar cheese, then with a tomato slice. Sprinkle salt and pepper to taste over the tomato, then sprinkle on a pinch of thyme and about 1 teaspoon of Parmesan cheese.

3. Bake for about 15 minutes. Let cool for 2 to 3 minutes before serving.

MAKES ABOUT 2 DOZEN TARTS, DEPENDING ON THE SIZE
OF THE BISCUIT CUTTER

Wonton Cheese Crisps

My editor, Sydny Miner, shared this super-easy recipe with me. The combination of ingredients may strike you as unusual, but you won't believe how fast these little bites come together, and how absolutely delicious they are. They're perfect when unexpected guests drop by. The recipe can be cut or expanded to meet your needs, and Sydny says she's even made it in the toaster oven!

You can use any cheese or combination of cheeses that appeals to you, and vary the accompanying garnish accordingly. I love a mix of mozzarella and Parmesan with marinara sauce, or a Mexican blend with spicy salsa.

One package of wonton skins has about 70 pieces, more than enough for this recipe. They will keep, well wrapped in plastic wrap or in an airtight plastic bag, for several weeks in the refrigerator.

> *24 wonton skins*
> *1½ to 2 cups shredded cheese, sharp Cheddar and*
> *Swiss mixed*
> *Your favorite chutney, for garnish*

1. Preheat the oven to 350°F. Coat 2 mini muffin tins, including the tops, with cooking spray.
2. Carefully fit one wonton skin into each muffin cup,

making a cup. If the wonton skin tears, patch it with a piece of another skin. Fill each cup with about 1 tablespoon of cheese.

3. Place the muffin tins in the oven and bake for 8 to 10 minutes, until the wontons are brown and crispy and the cheese is melted.

4. Remove from the oven and let set for 2 to 3 minutes; serve hot with a dollop of chutney, or allow your guests to garnish their own.

MAKES 2 DOZEN CRISPS

Slice-and-Bake Cheese Straws

Many a Southern cook's reputation has been founded on cheese straws. These aren't made with a cookie press. Just roll the dough into a log using waxed paper, refrigerate, and slice as you would refrigerator cookies.

½ cup (1 stick) butter, softened
1 pound sharp Cheddar cheese, grated
1½ cups all-purpose flour
½ teaspoon baking powder
½ teaspoon salt
¼ teaspoon cayenne pepper

1. Combine the butter and cheese in a food processor. Sift together the flour, baking powder, salt, and cayenne and add to the food processor bowl. Pulse until the dough forms a ball. Turn out onto waxed paper and roll into small logs. (I make several small ones for ease of handling.) Wrap each log in waxed paper and twist the ends to keep airtight. Refrigerate until firm enough to slice.

2. Preheat the oven to 350°F. Line cookie sheets with parchment paper or nonstick baking mats, or use nonstick sheets.

3. Cut the dough into ¼-inch slices and place ½ inch apart on the prepared cookie sheets. Bake for 12 to 15 minutes, until lightly browned. Let cool completely before placing into airtight containers. The dough may be placed into resealable plastic freezer bags and frozen. Baked cheese straws may be frozen. To reheat, place the frozen cheese straws in a 300°F oven for 5 minutes.

MAKES 8 DOZEN

Pink Shrimp Dip

*This dip has a great flavor and a beautiful pink color.
Serve it with crackers.*

> Two 8-ounce packages cream cheese, softened
> 2 teaspoons prepared horseradish
> Dash of Worcestershire sauce
> ½ cup seafood cocktail sauce (store-bought or
>   homemade, using your favorite recipe)
> 1 pound shrimp, boiled, peeled, deveined, and
>   coarsely chopped

Combine the cream cheese, horseradish, Worcestershire
sauce, and cocktail sauce in a medium bowl. Blend well.
Stir in the shrimp. Refrigerate, covered, until serving
time.

SERVES 12 TO 16

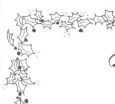

Egg Caviar Mold

4 hard-boiled eggs

5 tablespoons butter, softened

⅓ cup chopped green onions, green and white parts

⅓ cup mayonnaise

½ teaspoon fresh lemon juice

¼ cup sour cream

One 4-ounce or two 2-ounce jars caviar

In a food processor, combine the eggs, butter, onions, mayonnaise, and lemon juice, and process until well blended. Fill a small greased mold with this mixture and refrigerate for at least 3 hours. Turn the mold out onto a platter. Spread sour cream over and then sprinkle caviar on top. Serve with buttery crackers (I like Waverly Wafers) or toast points.

SERVES 4 TO 6

Cheese-Stuffed Mushrooms

24 fresh mushrooms, stems removed

One 10-ounce package frozen chopped
　　spinach, thawed

2 ounces cream cheese, softened

4 ounces feta cheese, crumbled (about 1 cup)

½ cup finely chopped green onions, green
　　and white parts

Salt

1 cup freshly grated Parmesan cheese

1. Preheat the oven to 350°F. Wipe the mushroom caps
with a damp paper towel. Drain the spinach in a colander
and squeeze out as much moisture as possible.

2. In a medium bowl, combine the spinach, cream
cheese, feta cheese, green onions, and salt to taste. Mix
well. Fill the mushroom caps with the mixture and place
on a cookie sheet. Sprinkle the Parmesan cheese on top.
Bake for 15 to 20 minutes until golden. Serve warm.

MAKES 2 DOZEN MUSHROOMS

Bacon Wraps

1 cup freshly grated Parmesan cheese

2 teaspoons garlic salt or powder

12 slices bacon

Twenty-four 4½-inch-long sesame breadsticks
(1 package)

1. Preheat the oven to 350°F. Line a cookie sheet with parchment paper.

2. Mix the Parmesan cheese with the garlic salt in a shallow bowl and set aside. Cut the bacon in half crosswise so that each piece is approximately 5 inches long. Wrap a piece of bacon around a breadstick, starting at one end of the breadstick and finishing at the other end. (I find that bacon adheres to sesame breadsticks better than to plain breadsticks.) Place on the cookie sheet. Repeat this process, using all of the breadsticks. Bake for about 15 minutes, until the bacon is browned and crisp. Remove from the cookie sheet and immediately roll the bacon wraps in the cheese mixture. Let cool and serve at room temperature.

MAKES 2 DOZEN

Pecan-Stuffed Dates

So good! This recipe has been around forever. Michael and I were recently guests of Billy and Katie Lee Joel (Katie Lee is writing her own cookbook). Katie Lee served these before dinner—which was meatloaf and mashed potatoes. She substituted whole roasted almonds for the pecans.

> One 8-ounce box pitted dates
> 30 pecan halves
> 10 to 12 slices bacon

1. Preheat the oven to 400°F. Line a cookie sheet with parchment paper.

2. Stuff each date with a pecan half. Cut each slice of bacon into three pieces. Wrap one piece around each stuffed date and secure with a toothpick. Bake until the bacon is browned and crisp, 12 to 15 minutes. Drain and serve.

MAKES APPROXIMATELY 30 DATES

Southern Holiday Pecans

These sweet and spicy nuts are fast, easy, and absolutely irresistible. I like to serve them warm from the oven.

2 cups pecan halves

3 tablespoons unsalted butter

¼ teaspoon cayenne pepper, or ½ teaspoon hot sauce

1 teaspoon ground cinnamon

1 tablespoon sugar

1 teaspoon salt

1. Preheat the oven to 325°F. Line a rimmed baking sheet with foil and spray with vegetable oil cooking spray. Place the pecans in a large heatproof bowl.

2. Melt the butter in a small saucepan and add the cayenne or hot sauce and cinnamon, and stir until combined. Pour over the pecans and toss until the nuts are completely coated. Sprinkle the sugar and salt over the pecans and toss again.

3. Spread the pecans on the prepared sheet in a single layer and bake for 15 minutes, stirring once. Cool on the baking sheet for 5 minutes and serve warm or at room temperature. Leftovers (if you have any!) can be stored in an airtight container for 3 to 5 days.

MAKES 2 CUPS

Sugar 'n' Spice

This recipe comes from Pam Strickland, owner of River Street Sweets in Savannah. No Christmas table in the South is complete without Sugar 'n' Spice pecans.

¾ cup light corn syrup

2 pounds sugar

2 teaspoons ground cinnamon

3 pounds pecan halves

1. Combine the corn syrup, sugar, and 1 cup water in a large heavy saucepan. Stir the mixture only until the sugar is completely moist. Place the saucepan over medium heat and cook until the mixture reaches 242°F (firm ball stage). At that point, immediately remove from the heat and add the cinnamon. Stir with a long-handled wooden spoon until the syrup settles or stops boiling.

2. Stir the pecan halves into the syrup all at once. Stir until all the pecans are coated completely and begin to separate from one another, and the sugar crystallizes. When the pecans are completely separated, pour out onto a cookie sheet and allow them to cool. Store in an airtight container.

MAKES 3 POUNDS

Hot Cranberry Cider

This smells so good when it's percolating. Once you've used your coffeepot to make it, however, it always has the smell of cloves and cinnamon sticks in it! We recommend you dedicate a cheap percolator to this recipe.

> ¼ cup packed brown sugar
>
> 3 cinnamon sticks, plus additional sticks to use
>   as stirrers
>
> 1 tablespoon whole cloves
>
> 6 cups cranberry juice cocktail
>
> 2 quarts apple juice

Put the sugar, cinnamon sticks, and cloves in the basket of a large coffee percolator. Put the juices in the bottom of the percolator. Bring to a boil over medium heat. Let the mixture perk as if making coffee. Serve with cinnamon stick stirrers, if desired.

MAKES 3½ QUARTS, ABOUT 18 SERVINGS

Apple Martini

*D*on't ask me why, but martinis are all the rage in our bar at The Lady & Sons restaurant in Savannah. Core and thinly slice green and red apples, and sprinkle them with lemon juice so they don't discolor. Perched on the edge of the glass, they make a pretty holiday garnish.

1½ ounces Absolut vodka

1¼ ounces Sour Apple Pucker schnapps liqueur

Dash of Cointreau

Shake like crazy with ½ cup crushed ice until only slivers of ice are left. Strain into a martini glass.

MAKES 1 DRINK

Cakes, Pies, Cupcakes, Puddings, and More Sweet Things

Gettin' a Christmas kiss from my handsome boys,
Jamie (on the left) and Bobby (on the right).

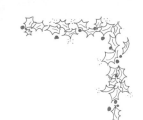

$\mathscr{I}$ don't know who said that you don't remember what you had for dinner, but you always remember what you had for dessert. Ain't that the truth!

My family does love their desserts, and in my house a meal's not a meal without something sweet at the end. 'Course, a cup of tea and a piece of cake in the afternoon, or a piece of pie late at night while we're watching a movie, goes down pretty easy, too.

I'm not a big fan of the traditional dark fruitcake, but I think it often gets a bad rap. My momma and grandmomma always made a fruitcake for the holidays, placing a small open container of brandy in the center of the cake. The cake would absorb the brandy flavor as it aged. I remember opening the lid of one of the tins of fruitcake and smelling the wonderful aroma. By the time you ate the last slice, it would knock your socks off!

When You're Baking:

1. When in doubt, sift flour before measuring.

2. To prevent those pesty little weevils from hatching in your unused meal or flour, place a few whole bay leaves in the container. Storing unused flour in the freezer or refrigerator will also help prevent their hatching.

3. When you buy flour, transfer it into an airtight container for storage, along with a piece of paper identifying the product. You definitely don't want to confuse your all-purpose flour with the self-rising variety.

4. When cooking or baking in glass pans, reduce the oven temperature by 25°F.

5. An average-sized lemon yields about 3 tablespoons juice and 1 tablespoon zest.

6. An average orange yields half a cup of juice.

7. To remove nutmeats whole from the shell, soak the nuts overnight in salted water before cracking them.

8. You will get a darker color and more mellow flavor from Dutch process versus regular cocoa.

Either type can be used in a recipe calling for cocoa.

9. Most of the recipe instructions call for greased and floured pans. I use Pam or Baker's Joy, a fat-free cooking spray. If you don't use these, grease your pans with a solid shortening instead of oil.

10. There are several ways to determine if a cake is done:

    • When you touch the center with your finger, the cake should spring back.

    • A toothpick, clean broom straw, or metal skewer inserted in the center comes out clean.

    • The cake begins to pull ever so slightly away from the sides of the pan.

11. Try to avoid opening the oven door to peek until the minimum cooking time is up.

12. Allow cakes to cool in the pan 5 to 10 minutes before inverting onto a cooling rack. If you have a stubborn cake, sit the cake pan on a wet, ice-cold kitchen towel for a minute or two, invert, and tap a few times on the bottom.

13. Before baking a layer cake, fill the pans, hold

3 or 4 inches from a hard, flat surface, and drop onto the surface several times. This allows air bubbles to escape and helps to produce a more even, level cake.

14. Store the cake in an airtight container. Once the cake has been sliced, you may want to press a piece of waxed paper or tinfoil against cut sides to help prevent staling.

15. To "fix" an overbaked cake, make a simple syrup of equal parts water and sugar along with a teaspoonful of flavoring (lemon, vanilla, maple, coconut, etc.) or a tablespoonful or two of a liqueur (rum or brandy). Bring to a boil, remove from the heat, and allow to cool. Pierce cake layers with a fork and brush each with the amount of syrup you think it needs. If this doesn't correct the texture, don't despair—cut the cake up into pieces and use in a trifle recipe. See Strawberry Delight (page 194) and Chocolate Delight (page 195) for ideas.

Perfect Measurements:

1. When you're baking, accuracy is of the utmost importance.
2. Never hold measuring spoons over the mixing bowl while measuring. If you accidentally over-pour something, such as salt, you could ruin your dish and have to start all over again.
3. When measuring sticky things like syrup, honey, or jelly, spray the measuring cup with a vegetable oil cooking spray. Almost every drop will come out with ease.
4. Do not use your flatware set (teaspoon or table-spoon) for measuring. Use only proper measuring spoons, except when dropping cookie dough onto the baking sheet.
5. If a recipe calls for "X cups sifted flour," that means to sift flour *before* measuring. If it calls for "X cups flour, sifted," sift the flour *after* measuring.

Coconut Pound Cake with 7-Minute Frosting

I always make a coconut cake for Christmas, always frosted with this fluffy frosting or with whipped cream and coconut, and decorated with holly sprigs.

2 cups (4 sticks) butter, softened

2 cups sugar

2 cups all-purpose flour

6 eggs

One 7-ounce package sweetened flaked coconut
  (2⅔ cups)

1 teaspoon vanilla extract

Glaze:

1 cup sugar

1 teaspoon coconut extract

7-Minute Frosting

1. Preheat the oven to 350°F. Generously grease and flour a 10-inch springform tube pan.

2. Cream the butter and sugar with an electric mixer. Add 1 cup of the flour and mix well. Add the eggs, one at

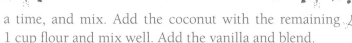

a time, and mix. Add the coconut with the remaining 1 cup flour and mix well. Add the vanilla and blend.

3. Pour the batter into the prepared pan. Bang the pan on the counter a couple of times to get rid of any air bubbles. Bake the cake for 1 hour and 15 minutes.

4. Remove the cake from the oven and set aside to cool for about 10 minutes. Meanwhile, make the glaze: In a small saucepan, simmer the sugar with ½ cup water until the sugar has dissolved, about 10 minutes. Stir in the coconut extract.

5. Run a knife around the outside edge of the cake. Remove the outer rim from the tube pan. While the cake is still hot, prick the top with the tines of a fork, and spoon the glaze over the top. Cool the cake on a wire rack.

6. Run the knife around the inner tube of the pan and under the bottom of the cake to loosen it. Take a plate and invert the cake onto it. Remove the bottom of the pan, then turn the cake back over so that the glazed part is on top. When completely cool, you can ice with 7-Minute Frosting. Store in an airtight container and serve at room temperature.

MAKES 12 TO 16 SERVINGS

7-Minute Frosting

2 egg whites
2 teaspoons light corn syrup

Dash of salt

1 teaspoon vanilla extract

⅓ cup toasted coconut, for garnish

Place the egg whites, corn syrup, salt, and ½ cup cold water into the top of a double boiler. With a handheld electric mixer, whip the ingredients for 1 minute. Cook over gently boiling water, beating with the electric mixer on high speed, until the frosting forms stiff peaks, about 7 minutes. Remove the top of the double boiler and add the vanilla to the frosting. Continue beating the frosting for 2 minutes more, until the frosting reaches spreading consistency. Frost the top and sides of the cooled coconut cake, then sprinkle with the toasted coconut.

I like to use greenery and fresh fruit at Christmas. Use whatever looks fresh and pretty, either from your garden or the florist. Use the fresh fruit of the season—oranges and limes and other citrus, and apples, and nuts, all different kinds. I love big bowls of oranges that have been studded with whole cloves—they smell so good when people walk in. Hollow out artichokes and put a nice pillar candle in the center. Make bundles of asparagus tied together with raffia, with a tapered candle in the center, and place up and down the dining table. These are just beautiful!

Southwest Georgia Pound Cake

My momma had several different pound cake recipes, but I think this was probably one of our favorites. This cake is great topped with fresh strawberries and vanilla ice cream, and (if you want it to be really good) topped with a dollop of fresh sweetened whipped cream. I promise you won't find a better strawberry shortcake anywhere. This is also wonderful sliced, buttered, and toasted for breakfast along with a spoonful of preserves, jelly, or jam. And don't forget a cup of good hot coffee.

1 cup (2 sticks) butter, softened

3 cups sugar

6 eggs

3 cups all-purpose flour

½ teaspoon baking powder

½ teaspoon salt

1 cup whipping cream

2 teaspoons vanilla extract (you may use lemon or
   almond flavoring instead)

1. Generously grease and flour a 10-inch Bundt pan.

2. Using an electric mixer, cream the butter and sugar together until fluffy. Add the eggs one at a time, beating well after each addition. Sift together the flour, baking powder, and salt. Alternately add the flour mixture and cream to the butter-sugar-egg mixture, beginning and ending with the flour. Stir in the flavoring. Pour the batter into the prepared pan.

3. Place in a cold oven and set the oven temperature at 325°F. Bake for 1¼ hours without opening the oven door. Bake for an additional 15 minutes if necessary. Remove from the oven and let cool in the pan for 15 minutes. Invert the cake onto a cake plate, and for a real treat, serve yourself a slice while it's still warm.

SERVES 16 TO 20

When baking a dense cake such as a pound cake, be careful not to overbeat. This type of cake can actually be beaten by hand, if you prefer.

Applesauce Cake

This is delicious with a scoop of vanilla ice cream.

> 1 cup granulated sugar
>
> ½ cup vegetable shortening
>
> 2 eggs
>
> 2 cups all-purpose flour
>
> 1 teaspoon ground cinnamon
>
> ½ teaspoon ground cloves
>
> ½ teaspoon freshly grated nutmeg
>
> 1 tablespoon baking powder
>
> ½ teaspoon salt
>
> 1 cup chopped nuts
>
> 1 cup raisins
>
> 1 cup unsweetened applesauce
>
> Confectioners' sugar, for sprinkling

1. Preheat the oven to 350°F. Grease a 13 by 9 by 2-inch baking pan.

2. Cream together the granulated sugar and shortening until fluffy, using an electric mixer. Add the eggs one at a time, beating well. In another bowl, sift together the flour, cinnamon, cloves, nutmeg, baking powder, and salt. Stir the nuts and raisins into the flour mixture.

3. Add the flour mixture and applesauce alternately to the creamed mixture, beginning and ending with the flour. Pour the batter into the prepared pan. Bake for 45 minutes or until the center of the cake is firm to the touch. Sprinkle with confectioners' sugar.

SERVES 16 TO 20

Jamie's Coconut Cake

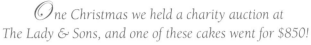

*One Christmas we held a charity auction at
The Lady & Sons, and one of these cakes went for $850!*

CAKE:

1 cup (2 sticks) butter, softened

2 cups sugar

4 eggs

3 cups sifted self-rising flour

1 cup canned unsweetened coconut milk

1 teaspoon vanilla extract

FILLING:

¾ cup sugar

1 cup sour cream

¼ cup milk

½ cup flaked, sweetened coconut

7-MINUTE FROSTING:

1½ cups sugar

¼ teaspoon cream of tartar or 1 tablespoon light
    corn syrup

⅛ teaspoon salt

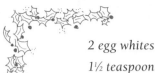

2 egg whites

1½ teaspoons vanilla extract

Flaked, sweetened coconut, for sprinkling

1. Preheat the oven to 350°F. Grease and flour three 9-inch round cake pans.

2. Using an electric mixer, cream the butter until fluffy. Add the sugar and continue to cream well for 6 to 8 minutes. Add the eggs one at a time, beating well after each addition. Add the flour and coconut milk alternately to the creamed mixture, beginning and ending with the flour. Add the vanilla and continue to beat until just mixed. Divide the batter equally among the prepared pans. Level the batter in each pan by holding the pan 3 or 4 inches above the counter, then dropping it flat onto the counter. Do this several times to release air bubbles and assure you of a more level cake. Bake for 25 minutes or until golden brown.

3. While the cake is baking, prepare the filling. Stir together the sugar, sour cream, milk, and coconut in a small bowl until well blended.

4. Remove the cake layers from the oven and allow the cake to remain in the pans as you prepare to stack and fill. Let cool for 5 to 10 minutes. Remove the first layer and invert it onto a cake plate. Using the handle end of a wooden spoon, poke holes approximately 1 inch apart until the entire layer has been poked. Spread one half of the filling mixture on the cake layer.

4. Top with the second layer and repeat poking and spreading. Top with the last layer and repeat the process again. (As I stack the layers together, I stick them with toothpicks to prevent the cake from shifting.)

5. To prepare the 7-Minute Frosting, place the sugar, cream of tartar, salt, ⅓ cup water, and egg whites in the top of a double boiler. Beat with a handheld electric mixer for 1 minute. Place the pan over boiling water, being sure that boiling water does not touch the bottom of the top pan. (If this happens, it could cause your frosting to become grainy.) Beat constantly on high speed with the electric mixer for 7 minutes. Beat in the vanilla. Frost the top and sides of the cake. Sprinkle the top and sides of the cakes with coconut.

SERVES 16 TO 20

Bobby's Caramel Cake

CAKE:

1 cup (2 sticks) butter, softened

2 cups granulated sugar

4 eggs

3 cups sifted self-rising flour

1 cup milk

1 teaspoon vanilla extract

FILLING:

1 cup (2 sticks) butter

2 cups packed light brown sugar

¼ cup milk

1 teaspoon vanilla extract

FROSTING:

½ cup (1 stick) butter

1 cup packed dark brown sugar

⅓ cup whipping cream, or more as necessary

One 16-ounce package confectioners' sugar

1 teaspoon vanilla extract

1 cup chopped nuts (optional)

1. Preheat the oven to 350°F. Grease and flour three 9-inch round cake pans.

2. Using an electric mixer, cream the butter until fluffy. Add the granulated sugar and continue to cream well for 6 to 8 minutes. Add the eggs one at a time, beating well after each addition. Add the flour and milk alternately to the creamed mixture, beginning and ending with the flour. Add the vanilla and continue to beat until just mixed. Divide the batter equally among the prepared pans. Level the batter in each pan by holding the pan 3 or 4 inches above the counter, then dropping it flat onto the counter. Do this several times to release air bubbles and assure you of a more level cake. Bake for 25 minutes or until golden brown.

3. Meanwhile, prepare the cake filling. In a medium saucepan, combine the butter, brown sugar, and milk. Cook and stir over medium heat for 3 to 5 minutes. Remove from the heat and stir in the vanilla.

4. Remove the cake layers from the oven and allow the cake to remain in the pans as you prepare to stack and fill. Let cool for 5 to 10 minutes. Remove the first layer and invert it onto a cake plate. Pierce the cake layer with a toothpick over the entire surface. Spread one half of the filling on the cake layer. Top with the second layer and repeat poking and spreading. Top with the last layer. (As I stack the layers together, I stick them with toothpicks to prevent the cake from shifting.)

5. To prepare the frosting, melt the butter in a saucepan over medium heat and stir in the brown sugar and

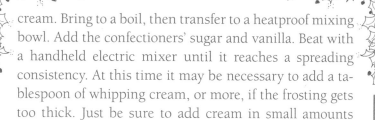

cream. Bring to a boil, then transfer to a heatproof mixing bowl. Add the confectioners' sugar and vanilla. Beat with a handheld electric mixer until it reaches a spreading consistency. At this time it may be necessary to add a tablespoon of whipping cream, or more, if the frosting gets too thick. Just be sure to add cream in small amounts because you can always "add to" but you can't take away. Frost the top and sides of the cake and sprinkle the top with chopped nuts, if desired.

SERVES 16 TO 20

A pinch of salt added to the sugar when making icings will prevent graining.

Grandmomma Paul's Japanese Fruitcake

When I was a child, Christmas didn't come to our house or Grandmomma Paul's house without one of these big beautiful cakes on the counter. I sometimes frost this cake at the last minute with a 7-Minute Frosting (page 161).

CAKE:

1 cup vegetable shortening

2 cups sugar

4 eggs

3 cups sifted all-purpose flour

2 teaspoons baking powder

1 teaspoon salt

1 cup milk

1 teaspoon vanilla extract

SPICE LAYER:

1 teaspoon ground cinnamon

½ teaspoon ground cloves

1 teaspoon ground allspice

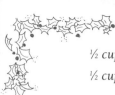

½ cup raisins, dusted with a little flour
½ cup coarsely chopped nuts

FILLING AND TOPPING:

2 cups sugar
2 tablespoons cornstarch
1 cup boiling water
One 20-ounce can crushed pineapple, drained
1 cup grated coconut
Juice and zest of 2 lemons
½ cup maraschino cherry halves

1. Preheat the oven to 350°F. Grease and flour three 9-inch round cake pans.

2. Using an electric mixer, cream together the shortening and sugar until fluffy. Add the eggs one at a time, beating well after each addition. Stir together the flour, baking powder, and salt in another bowl. Add the flour mixture alternately with the milk to the creamed mixture, beginning and ending with the flour. Add the vanilla and mix well.

3. Divide the batter into thirds. Pour one third into each of two prepared pans. To the remaining one third of the batter, add the spice layer ingredients, folding in well. Pour into the remaining prepared pan. Bake for 25 to 30 minutes. Let cool in the pans for 10 minutes, then invert onto a wire rack to cool completely.

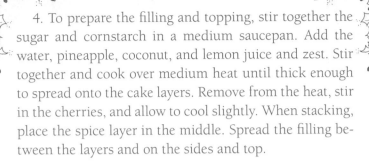

4. To prepare the filling and topping, stir together the sugar and cornstarch in a medium saucepan. Add the water, pineapple, coconut, and lemon juice and zest. Stir together and cook over medium heat until thick enough to spread onto the cake layers. Remove from the heat, stir in the cherries, and allow to cool slightly. When stacking, place the spice layer in the middle. Spread the filling between the layers and on the sides and top.

SERVES 16 TO 20

Almond Cups

One 8-ounce can Solo pure almond paste
2 eggs
½ cup (1 stick) butter, melted, then cooled
Chocolate chips, fresh pineapple slices, or dried
*   cherries or blueberries*

1. Preheat the oven to 350°F. Spray mini muffin tins with vegetable oil cooking spray.

2. Place the almond paste, eggs, and butter in a food processor and mix until well blended, smooth, and lump free. Fill the muffin tins three-quarters full with almond mixture. Top with chocolate chips, pineapple, or dried cherries or blueberries. Bake for 18 minutes or until golden.

MAKE 2 DOZEN MINI CUPS

Old South Jelly Roll Cake

4 eggs, separated

¾ cup granulated sugar

1 tablespoon vanilla extract

¾ cup sifted cake flour

¾ teaspoon baking powder

¼ teaspoon salt

*Confectioners' sugar, sifted, for dusting, plus some
    for sprinkling*

1 cup jam or jelly, stirred well

Whipped cream, for garnish

1. Preheat the oven to 400°F. Line a 15 by 10 by 1-inch jelly roll pan with waxed paper.

2. In a small bowl, beat the egg whites until stiff but not dry; set aside. In another bowl, beat the egg yolks until light; gradually add the granulated sugar and vanilla. Sift together the flour, baking powder, and salt; mix gently into the egg-yolk mixture. Fold in the egg whites and pour the batter into the prepared pan. Bake for 8 to 10 minutes or until light brown.

3. Loosen the edges of the cake, then invert the cake onto a lint-free, clean kitchen towel dusted with confec-

tioners' sugar (this will prevent the cake from sticking to the towel).

4. Gently peel the waxed paper from the cake. Trim ¼ inch of hard crust off each long side of the jelly roll cake (this will allow you to roll the cake without it splitting). Beginning with the narrow end, roll up the cake and towel together. Let the cake cool on a wire rack, seam side down, for 10 to 15 minutes. Gently unroll and spread the cake with jam and reroll. Sprinkle with confectioners' sugar or spread with whipped cream.

SERVES 8 TO 10

To ensure an easy roll on jelly roll cakes, it may be necessary to trim the crisp edges off with a serrated knife. This will prevent the cake from splitting or cracking as you roll it up.

 Plum Cake

1 cup vegetable oil

2 cups granulated sugar

3 eggs

1 teaspoon ground cloves

1 teaspoon ground cinnamon

2 cups self-rising flour

Two 4-ounce jars strained plum baby food with
    tapioca

1 cup chopped pecans

GLAZE:

1 cup confectioners' sugar

Juice of 1 lemon

1. Preheat the oven to 350°F. Grease and flour a 10-inch Bundt pan.

2. Mix the oil, granulated sugar, eggs, cloves, cinnamon, flour, and baby food in a large bowl with an electric mixer. Beat at medium speed for 3 to 4 minutes. Stir in the pecans. Pour into the prepared pan. Bake for 1 hour and 10 minutes. Remove from the oven and allow to cool for 10 minutes.

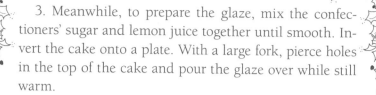

3. Meanwhile, to prepare the glaze, mix the confectioners' sugar and lemon juice together until smooth. Invert the cake onto a plate. With a large fork, pierce holes in the top of the cake and pour the glaze over while still warm.

SERVES 16 TO 18

Cheesecake Cupcakes

These taste just like miniature cheesecakes without the crust. Decorate with fresh seasonal fruit—a sliver of strawberry (if available) or kiwi for Christmas, or a dollop of fruit topping or jam. You can eat about a dozen, so be careful.

Three 8-ounce packages cream cheese, softened
1 cup sugar
4 eggs
1½ teaspoons vanilla extract

TOPPING:

1 cup sour cream
¼ cup sugar
1 teaspoon vanilla extract
Kiwi or strawberry slivers, fruit topping, or jam

1. Preheat the oven to 325°F. Line 24 regular muffin cups with paper cupcake liners.

2. In a large mixing bowl, beat the cream cheese until very smooth. Add the sugar and mix well. Add the eggs and vanilla and mix well.

3. Fill the cups about half full with the batter. Bake for about 25 minutes, until the cupcakes are set and golden brown.

4. Make the topping: Combine the sour cream, sugar, and vanilla and stir well with a metal spoon or spatula. Spoon about 2 teaspoons on top of each cupcake and return to the oven for 5 minutes to glaze.

5. Remove the cupcakes from the oven. When they can be handled safely, remove them from the muffin tins and let cool completely on wire racks. When completely cool, place them in plastic containers with lids and refrigerate until ready to serve. Just before serving, decorate with slivers of freshly cut seasonal fruit, or jam or fruit topping. Serve at room temperature.

MAKES 2 DOZEN

Peanut Butter Brownie Cupcakes

Make these any time you're asked to "bring brownies." They are so pretty, and people love it when they hit the peanut butter.

One 21-ounce package Duncan Hines Family Style
Chewy Fudge Brownie Mix
One 10- to 11-ounce package peanut butter chips or
24 miniature peanut butter cups

1. Preheat the oven to 350°F. Line 24 regular muffin cups with paper cupcake liners.

2. Prepare the brownie mix according to package directions for cakelike brownies. Fill the cups half full with brownie batter. Place about 1 tablespoon peanut butter chips in the center of the batter, or press 1 peanut butter cup into the batter in each muffin cup until the batter meets the top edge of the peanut butter cup. Bake for 18 to 20 minutes, until the cupcakes are set.

3. When they can be handled safely, remove the cupcakes from the muffin tins and let cool completely on wire racks. Store in an airtight container.

MAKES 2 DOZEN

Apple Butter Pumpkin Pie

This pie recipe was given to me by June Royals Foster in loving memory of her mother, Virgie Royals. June says it's wonderful served slightly warm with sweetened fresh whipped cream.

1 cup apple butter

1 cup mashed cooked fresh or canned pumpkin

½ cup packed brown sugar

½ teaspoon salt

¾ teaspoon ground cinnamon

¾ teaspoon freshly grated nutmeg

⅛ teaspoon ground ginger

3 eggs, slightly beaten

¾ cup evaporated milk

1 unbaked 9-inch piecrust, fitted into a 9-inch metal pie plate

Sweetened whipped cream, for garnish (optional)

1. Preheat the oven to 425°F.

2. Combine the apple butter, pumpkin, sugar, salt, and spices in a bowl. Stir in the eggs. Gradually add the milk and mix well. Pour into the piecrust. Bake for about 40 minutes, until set. Cut into wedges. Garnish with whipped cream, if desired.

SERVES 6

Bob's Peppermint Pie

This recipe makes the nostalgic candy table-ready as a dessert that you and your inner child will love.

> 1 envelope unflavored gelatin
> ½ cup whipping cream
> 8 ounces soft peppermint candy
> 1½ cups whipping cream, whipped
> 1 chocolate cookie crust
> Crushed peppermint candy

Soften the gelatin in ¼ cup cold water and set aside. Combine the ½ cup cream and the candy in a small saucepan and cook over low heat until the candy melts. Add the gelatin and mix well. Let cool and fold in the whipped cream. Pour into the crust, sprinkle with crushed peppermint candy, and chill.

MAKES 1 PIE

Christmas Nut Pie

*Perfect for the harried holiday rush
and the Christmas Eve table.*

½ cup (1 stick) butter, melted

1 cup sugar

⅛ teaspoon salt

2 eggs, lightly beaten

1 tablespoon white vinegar

½ cup flaked coconut

½ cup raisins

1 cup chopped walnuts

1 teaspoon vanilla extract

1 unbaked 9-inch piecrust, fitted into a 9-inch metal
   pie plate

1. Preheat the oven to 350°F.

2. Mix the butter, sugar, salt, eggs, vinegar, coconut, raisins, walnuts, and vanilla together in a large bowl until well blended. Pour into the piecrust and bake for 40 to 50 minutes, or until set.

SERVES 6 TO 8

Eggnog Pudding

This recipe was used to tempt a friend of mine as a small child; otherwise she would not have received the nutritional benefits of milk. This is still her favorite pudding after all these years.

¼ *cup all-purpose flour*

1 tablespoon cornstarch

¾ *cup sugar*

3 cups milk

2 eggs, separated

1 tablespoon butter

1 teaspoon vanilla extract

2 egg whites, stiffly beaten

Freshly grated nutmeg

1. Mix together the flour, cornstarch, and sugar in a saucepan; stir well. Add ½ cup of the milk to the flour mixture and stir until smooth. In another saucepan, scald the remaining 2½ cups milk (heat to just below the boiling point); add to the flour mixture. Cook and stir the mixture over medium-low heat; do not allow to boil. In a small bowl, beat the egg yolks. Remove ½ cup of the hot mixture and add to the yolks to temper them; mix well and return to the saucepan. Continue to cook over low

heat for an additional 2 to 3 minutes. Remove from the heat. Stir in the butter and vanilla.

2. Beat the egg whites with an electric mixer until stiff but not dry. Thoroughly fold the egg whites into the hot mixture. Place in individual dessert dishes, sprinkle tops with nutmeg, and chill. If you wish, you may serve this from a single bowl.

SERVES 6 TO 8

The Best Bread Pudding

On September 20, 2000, Joanie Duke, one of the cutest little older ladies that I've had the pleasure of meeting, bounded into the restaurant (and when I say "bounded in" I really mean it). She told me how much she enjoyed my recipes and that she had one of hers to share with me and shoved something into my hand, covered with plastic wrap. It was the best bread pudding I had ever wrapped my lips around. This quickly became the favorite bread pudding recipe for The Lady & Sons.

2 cups granulated sugar

5 large eggs, beaten

2 cups milk

2 teaspoons vanilla extract

3 cups cubed Italian bread, cut and allowed to stale overnight in a bowl

1 cup packed light brown sugar

¼ cup (½ stick) butter, softened

1 cup chopped pecans

SAUCE:

1 cup granulated sugar

½ cup (1 stick) butter, melted

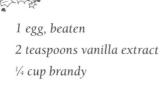

1 egg, beaten

2 teaspoons vanilla extract

¼ cup brandy

1. Preheat the oven to 350°F. Grease a 13 by 9 by 2-inch baking pan.

2. Mix together the granulated sugar, eggs, and milk in a large bowl; add the vanilla. Pour over the cubed bread and let sit for 10 minutes. In another bowl, mix and crumble together the brown sugar, butter, and pecans. Pour the bread mixture into the prepared pan. Sprinkle the brown sugar mixture over the top and bake for 35 to 45 minutes, or until set. Remove from the oven.

3. Make the sauce: Mix together the sugar, butter, egg, and vanilla in a saucepan. Over medium heat, stir together until the sugar is melted. Add the brandy, stirring well. Pour over the bread pudding. Delicious served warm or cold.

SERVES 8 TO 10

I've found sticking the bread in a 250°F oven for 10 to 15 minutes works just as well as staling the slices overnight.

Cassata Cake

This Italian dessert tastes something like a cake version of cannoli.

2 pounds ricotta cheese (I use Sorrento whole milk
   deli style.)
1½ cups confectioners' sugar
1 teaspoon vanilla extract
¼ cup white crème de cacao
¼ cup small semisweet chocolate chips
30 plain ladyfingers, split
1½ cups whipping cream
⅓ cup granulated sugar
Maraschino cherries and walnuts or pecans,
   for decorating

1. Combine the cheese, confectioners' sugar, vanilla, and crème de cacao in the bowl of an electric mixer. Beat at medium speed for about 10 minutes; the mixture should be fluffy. Stir in the chocolate chips. Line the bottom and sides of a 10-inch springform pan with ladyfingers. Pour in one third of the filling; top with ladyfingers. Repeat layers, using the remaining filling and ladyfingers. Refrigerate overnight.

2. When ready to serve, beat together the cream and granulated sugar with a handheld electric mixer until stiff peaks form. Frost the top of the cake with the whipped cream and decorate with cherries and nuts. Remove the ring from the springform pan before serving.

SERVES 10

Strawberry Delight

No need to make your own; store-bought angel food cake is fine. If you don't have a trifle bowl, any large glass bowl will do.

1 large angel food cake

One 8-ounce package cream cheese, softened

One 14-ounce can sweetened condensed milk, regular or fat-free

2 cups whipping cream

2 tablespoons sugar

Two 10-ounce packages frozen sweetened, halved strawberries, thawed

1. Cut the angel food cake into cubes about the size of a walnut. In a small mixing bowl, combine the cream cheese and sweetened condensed milk, mixing until smooth and completely blended. In a separate medium bowl, whip the cream with the sugar until stiff.

2. To assemble: In a trifle bowl, layer half the angel food cake cubes, cream cheese mixture, whipped cream, and strawberries. Repeat, layering the remaining ingredients, and ending with whipped cream and strawberries.

SERVES ABOUT 16

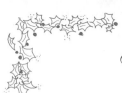

Chocolate Delight

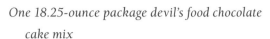

*One 18.25-ounce package devil's food chocolate
cake mix*

*Three 3.9-ounce packages regular instant chocolate
pudding mix (or 1.9-ounce sugar free)*

Milk

2 cups whipping cream

2 tablespoons sugar

1 cup chopped pecans, lightly toasted

Chocolate sauce or syrup, any variety, for garnish

1. Prepare the cake mix and bake in a 13 by 9-inch pan according to package directions. Let cool thoroughly, then cut into cubes about the size of a walnut.

2. Prepare the chocolate pudding with milk according to package directions.

3. In a medium bowl, using an electric mixer, whip the cream with the sugar until stiff.

4. To assemble: In a trifle bowl, layer half of the chocolate cake cubes, pudding, whipped cream, and nuts. Repeat, layering the remaining ingredients, ending with whipped cream and nuts.

5. Drizzle decoratively with chocolate sauce.

SERVES ABOUT 20

My Christmas Wish for You

That you keep and share the giving spirit of Christmas in your heart all year long.

Table of Weights and Measures

3 teaspoons	1 tablespoon
16 tablespoons	1 cup
2 tablespoons	⅛ cup
4 tablespoons	¼ cup
5⅓ tablespoons	⅓ cup
12 tablespoons	¾ cup
1 cup	½ pint
60 drops	1 teaspoon
2 cups	1 pint
2 pints	1 quart
16 ounces	1 pound
16 liquid ounces	1 pint

Metric Equivalencies

LIQUID EQUIVALENCIES

CUSTOMARY	METRIC
¼ teaspoon	1.25 milliliters
½ teaspoon	2.5 milliliters
1 teaspoon	5 milliliters
1 tablespoon	15 milliliters
1 fluid ounce	30 milliliters
¼ cup	60 milliliters
⅓ cup	80 milliliters
½ cup	120 milliliters
1 cup	240 milliliters
1 pint (2 cups)	480 milliliters
1 quart (4 cups)	960 milliliters (.96 liter)
1 gallon (4 quarts)	3.84 liters

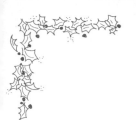

DRY MEASURE EQUIVALENCIES

CUSTOMARY	METRIC
1 ounce (by weight)	28 grams
¼ pound (4 ounces)	114 grams
1 pound (16 ounces)	454 grams
2.2 pounds	1 kilogram (1,000 grams)

OVEN TEMPERATURE EQUIVALENCIES

DESCRIPTION	°FAHRENHEIT	°CELSIUS
Cool	200	90
Very slow	250	120
Slow	300–325	150–160
Moderately slow	325–350	160–180
Moderate	350–375	180–190
Moderately hot	375–400	190–200
Hot	400–450	200–230
Very hot	450–500	230–260

Credits and Permissions

Recipes for Egg Caviar Mold (p. 145), Crème Fraîche Mashed Potatoes (p. 124), Sour Cream–Butter Biscuits (p. 84) , and Gorilla Bread (p. 104) are from *The Lady & Sons, Too!* by Paula H. Deen, copyright © 2000 by Paula H. Deen. Used by permission of Random House, Inc.

Recipes for Pecan-Stuffed Dates (p. 148), Cheese-Stuffed Mushrooms (p. 146), Bacon Wraps (p. 147), and Sweet Potato Bake (p. 126) are from *The Lady & Sons Savannah Country Cookbook* by Paula H. Deen, copyright © 1997, 1998 by Paula H. Deen; Introduction copyright © 1998 by John Berendt. Used by permission of Random House, Inc.

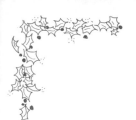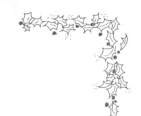

Index

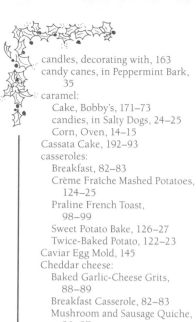